Growing Weed *in the* Garden

a No-Fuss, Seed-to-Stash Guide *to* Outdoor Cannabis Cultivation

Growing Weed *in the* Garden

a No-Fuss, Seed-to-Stash Guide *to* Outdoor Cannabis Cultivation

Johanna Silver
Photography by Rachel Weill

Abrams
New York

Dedicated
to
high school
Johanna

Contents

Full Transparency

I need to come clean to you. I am not a stoner. Though I spent the last two years of high school smoking pot at Robinson Park in Denver, Colorado, during lunch hour, that phase of life has passed. I'm barely a user. My brother in New York City, a weed lover if there ever was one, keeps my usage from falling off the map entirely when we get together.

That I'd ever write about cannabis was completely unexpected. I'd gotten laid off as garden editor of *Sunset* magazine in late 2017, and I had every intention to keep writing about plants. Included on my short list of contacts was Kitty Morgan, who had served as

A cannabis seedling at the very start of its journey.

editor in chief of *Sunset* during a stretch of my decade there. She had landed as the assistant managing editor of the *San Francisco Chronicle.* Kitty is fierce, creative, and a fantastic editor. I told her I'd love to write for her again, assuming the assignment would be something in my wheelhouse—backyard design, edible gardening, or container refreshes.

All roads in Mendocino, Humboldt, and Trinity Counties lead to weed—you just have to know where to look (and it's probably a good idea to secure your invitation first).

Instead, she told me she wanted me to grow weed in my backyard and document it as a gardener. "I don't even know where to get seeds," I told her. "That's your opening line!" she exclaimed.

Proposition 64, which made recreational cannabis use legal in California, was weeks away from going into effect, and the *Chronicle*, along with all other media, was confronted with how to tackle the subject in this new world.

My early googling quickly revealed that cannabis is dioecious, meaning there are separate male and female plants. This means not only do you have to learn how to "sex plants," a phrase that was enough to pique my interest, but also that a worthwhile crop relies on having no male plants in the garden. Do you know how rare dioecious crops are? Let me tell you: rare. Kiwi, asparagus, and spinach are all dioecious, but there is no other summer annual that fits the bill. Can you imagine starting your tomato seeds, having to learn to tell the difference between male and female plants, and then having to kill half of them? The nerdy gardener in me was hooked on that unique factor alone.

The plot thickens. At the time of writing, pot is projected to be a $5 billion industry in California alone, just behind dairy ($6 billion), almonds ($5.5 billion), and ahead of grapes ($5 billion). Yet it's never gone through a modern-day breeding program to select for things like disease resistance or seed stability. Again, mind blown. And its medicinal value—though heralded as being helpful for everything from pain to cancer—is barely understood. There is nothing else in the world so widely grown but so little understood and yet-to-be-studied.

As the project unfolded and I wrote for the *Chronicle*, I came to know a handful of farmers in Humboldt and Mendocino Counties (aka the Emerald Triangle—the region that produces the majority of the weed grown in the United States) and met families greatly impacted by the fact that this plant was illegal for the last one hundred years. It was at this point that I stopped regarding this project as a hilarious adventure and started taking it a bit more seriously. We're talking about people's stories, people's livelihoods, people's crafts. How this plant is written about and valued in our culture matters.

I ordered every cannabis book ever written as a supplement to my own research. What quickly became apparent is that they are written primarily for indoor

growers. They read like electrician handbooks, not gardening manuals. Any nod to outdoor cultivation is mostly about security concerns—what breed of dog barks loudest, what type of tape to line the soles of your shoes with to hide your tracks, and what type of fence is most private. Though I've grown to appreciate that these security concerns are a real issue for people growing in clandestine settings, those conditions didn't match my own.

I simply wanted to grow a few plants in my garden. Because I could. Easy-to-understand, jargon-free information was hard to find. I've written this book for anyone remotely curious about growing cannabis casually. I wasn't able to relay even a fraction of what I learned about the process of growing weed in my pieces for the newspaper, and that left me feeling like I had much more to share—specifically, accessible information for every step of the process, from cultivar selection to finished product. I also wanted to share profiles of some growers who each deepened my appreciation for the plant and proved that there's no one type of cannabis fan. I know the hunger for information is out there, and here you'll find it in full detail and accompanied by beautiful outdoor photography. I'm not interested in maximizing yields. I'm not buying expensive lights or odor-masking filters. I'm certainly not going to be buying any chemicals, which I've never done for anything I've grown (except houseplants—I will own up to using Miracle-Gro on houseplants). I include the simplest, most effective techniques that involve the least amount of equipment.

Here's the thing about learning to grow weed: If you learn from a pot-centric person, you're going to pick up a strange language. Prohibition forced breeding and growing underground—and indoors. You'll hear about *clones* and *strains* and *vegetative states*. That lingo a) makes the whole thing seem complicated, and b) doesn't translate well to any other plant you might want to grow (*clones* are otherwise called cuttings, *strains* is the wrong word for cultivars, and *vegetative state* just means growing).

Weed is unlike anything I've ever grown. Not because it's so complicated, but because it's fun—the smells are out of this world, it's sticky as can be, and it grows faster than all get-out. It's not the hardest thing you can grow. Spoiler alert: It's called *weed* for a reason.

I'm not a perfectionist. I'm not a control freak. I believe that gardening—weed or basil or tomatoes or peonies—should add richness to your life, not stress. I want this book to empower you and also to relax you, as I hope all gardening does. As my boss at the first farm I ever worked at told me over and over, "Plants want to grow." Have a little faith. You've got this.

One can't deny the visual appeal of cannabis leaves.

This project breathed life into me at a time when I didn't know what was next. I poured my heart and soul into it, as did my photographer, Rachel Weill. A wise woman once told me that you can always tell if a book was written by someone having fun. I sure as hell hope you have as much fun reading and using this one as we had making it.

Here's to bringing the conversation about cannabis out of the dark and into the light. Natural sunlight, preferably. Enjoy!

following
With plenty of sunshine, weed babies grow quickly.

Why Grow Pot ?

A love of getting high would be the obvious reason for growing weed in the garden. But what if you're so totally not a stoner and yet you are still oddly compelled to try your hand at growing weed?

You are not alone. You'd be surprised how many people grow weed for a reason other than their own consumption, be it an addiction to gardening or a desire to gift the harvest. Some farmers never touch the product, but inherited the livelihood from previous generations. Of course, I meet plenty of people who grow specifically to enjoy their harvest, too. But those

Dense clusters of female flowers form after the summer solstice. Unpollinated female flowers are your end goal when you grow weed.

reasons are just as varied, from treating chronic pain to channeling creativity to preferring a few hits over a few drinks to unwind.

If you are a user, dedicated or casual, there is ample reason to grow your own stash. As you know from farmers' markets or your own backyard plot of tomatoes, growing your own allows you to grow precisely the cultivar you want, harvest at peak freshness, control all inputs, and in the case of cannabis, benefit from some serious cost savings.

Outside, in full sun—the way nature intended for cannabis to grow. Here, a backyard cannabis plant mixes with maroon-leafed smoke bush, purple-flowering Mexican sage, and bursts of golden coreopsis.

In a pre-legalization landscape, your only option was to grow indoors or assume great risk outdoors. Indoor grows take an immense amount of dedication and precision. Lights, fans, and chemicals are all nonnegotiable components of an indoor "garden." I don't know about you, but a few plants in a tent with a bunch of fake light sure doesn't feel like a garden to me. In a world where prohibition is rapidly becoming a thing of the past, indoor grows aren't necessary. You can now grow plants outside—where plants want to grow! It doesn't have to be an expensive hobby that takes over a room in your house and increases your utility bill. You can grow it the lazy way, letting sunlight, fresh air, compost, and drip irrigation do most of the work.

Putting consumption aside entirely, there's reason to grow a plant just for the sake of the cultivating experience. As a gardener, I've enjoyed growing all sorts of crops that I don't necessarily find delicious. I hate eggplant but include them in the garden every year because I love watching the bulbous fruit turn glossy as it ripens. And I love experimenting with all of the different cultivars from around the world. I've grown skinny foot-long purple ones from Japan, lime-green golf-ball-size ones from Thailand, and white-and-purple-speckled, softball-size heirlooms from Italy. Regardless of the harvest, I get so much out of nurturing a plant and watching it express itself and complete its life cycle. Then I give them to my friend, Ben, to cook.

Cannabis is in that category for me (though I probably do enjoy it more than eggplant). I use it from time to time, but I'm more interested in growing it for the experience than for using the harvest. But there's something a little more significant about including cannabis in the garden than eggplant or peppers. Cannabis is among the oldest cultivated plants in the world, and while it's long been prized as food, for fibers, and as medicine and drug, it's been just as heavily demonized in the last century.

Prohibition in the United States began as a racist, fear-based response to immigration along our southern border. In the latter half of the twentieth century, the War on Drugs led the United States to have the highest incarceration rate in

ink flowers? It all ooks the same once t's dry. You've got o grow it yourself o catch the beauty long the way.

Into the Light

Currently, indoor weed sells for more than cannabis grown in the sun. While it's certainly more expensive to grow weed indoors (due to equipment and energy), consumers also largely value indoors to out, thinking that indoor weed is somehow better quality than that grown in nature. I believe this to be completely backward, and I look forward to this trend changing in time. Just like my tomatoes, I want something grown outdoors, bathed in natural sunlight, soaking up nutrients from the soil. I believe things grown outdoors taste better, and I support reducing the carbon footprint of agricultural products.

the world, disproportionately locking up people of color—a statistic that holds true today. The US government has wasted billions of dollars working to eradicate a plant that has never killed anyone. While legalization poses immense economic challenges to the cannabis community, it is a step in the right direction. And as such, it feels *important* to include cannabis in the garden as a statement of solidarity and normalization. I'm growing weed because I can.

While I hope to dispel the mysteriousness of the growing process, I bow to the mystique of the plant, whose properties we do not fully understand. We are but scratching the surface of the plant's potential, be it as medicine, recreation, or sacrament. I also humbly thank all those who have made serious sacrifices in the name of growing what they love. Including cannabis in the garden is one of the oldest activities you can partake in. And with legalization sweeping the land, my question to you is simply: Why not?

A Ridiculously Condensed History: *Weed's Wild Journey Around the Globe*

Chapter 1

The iconic cannabis leaf: serrated-edged leaflets radiating in a palmate pattern, if we're going to be technical.

Humans have been farming weed for as long as we've been farming. About ten thousand years ago, ice melt from the end of the last major ice age revealed fertile soil next to raging rivers. Under those conditions, humans figured out how to grow plants more intentionally—rather than exclusively hunting and gathering—near their settlements. They picked seeds of plants they liked, and thus the practice of human selection, or breeding, was born. Early farmers focused on the most useful plants—those that were productive, versatile, and nutritious. They included wheat, barley, lentils, peas, flax, and, yes—cannabis. In fact, increasing evidence suggests that cannabis might have been the first among those crops. This intentional cultivation led to surplus resources, allowing for trade, population growth, the accumulation of wealth and power, and the foundation for life in a post-hunter-gatherer world. In other words: Farming was a pretty big turning point for humankind, and weed was right there at the center.

Here's why: The plant grew readily in open spaces, full sun, and rich soil—exactly the type of environment found by hunter and gatherer camps. Second, every part of the plant was usable. From this fast-growing plant, we've gotten strong fibers, nutritious seeds, medicines, and drugs.

Today, most agree that cannabis is indigenous to central Asia. From there, we took seeds of the plant everywhere we went, and the plant adapted based on the double whammy of human selection and climatic conditions. Its first stops were the Himalayas of Afghanistan and into the Indian subcontinent. By 2000 BCE, we had taken it to Persia, Asia Minor, and Europe. And by 1500 CE, cannabis grew in Africa and Southeast Asia.

In northern climates of central Asia (specifically the Hindu Kush mountain range of Afghanistan and Pakistan), plants

were subjected to harsher climates and cold winters. Plants responded by growing shorter and squatter. Leaves grew wider and denser, often with purple highlights. We describe these plants as northern or indica types and consider their highs to be sedentary and relaxing.

As the plant continued its journey into equatorial regions, like Thailand, Mexico, Colombia, Peru, and parts of Africa, plants grew elongated in mild, frost-free conditions. Stalks grew taller and spindlier, with long, narrow leaves. We call these equatorial or sativa types; their highs are uplifting, cerebral, and good for creative endeavors.

Cannabis settled in each of these pockets of the world. Some regions focused on using the plant for psychoactive purposes, some on seed oil, and some on fibers. We use the term *landrace* to describe these regionalized cultivars of

Fast-growing and useful from stalk to seed, cannabis has been part of the human experience at least since we started farming, and some propose since we've learned to control fire.

What's in a Name: A Primer on Pot Lingo

cannabis
Refers to the entire genus and all of its uses, from drug to fiber. Many people within the legalization movement prefer this term, as it professionalizes the industry. Frankly, I find it a bit stiff.

marijuana, weed, ganja, pot
These are just a tiny sampling of slang names for cannabis cultivars with psychoactive components, aka the ones that get you high.

hemp
Historically refers to cannabis cultivars bred specifically for fibers to make into rope, paper, and textiles. These cultivars were tall, stalky plants that were low in sticky resin, which houses cannabinoids and terpenes (see page 41) that give drug or medicinal cultivars their power. The current legal definition of hemp is any cannabis plant containing less than .3 percent THC, a psychoactive cannabinoid, by dry weight. Cultivars of cannabis that are low in THC but high in CBD, a nonpsychoactive, potentially medicinal cannabinoid (see page 42), are often referred to as hemp, even though their intended use isn't for fiber and the varieties might be high in resin. It's a new application of a very old word.

botanically speaking
While taxonomists might not ever agree, geneticists do: There is but one species of cannabis, *C. sativa*. Hence, I refer to indica and sativa as types of cannabis having evolved under different climactic conditions, producing different effects, but not as separate species.

cannabis that adapted over time to both their ecological and cultural environments. If you're a gardener, you can think of landrace as a type of heirloom or heritage cultivar that comes from a certain part of the world.

As we crawl out from a THC-obsessed era of prohibition, nuanced landrace cultivars, having been bred for more complicated qualities than just a powerful high, could help us unlock the full range of cannabis genetics. Hunting for them and bringing them into production has the potential to aid our discovery of untouched qualities, but also could lead to exploitation of the people and ecology of specific locales if not done responsibly.

Meanwhile, *hemp* refers to cannabis cultivars low in THC and historically bred for fiber. Hemp plants resemble sativa types in that they're usually tall and spindly. It's thought that hemp types were established first in Eastern Europe, and by Roman times, hemp farming was a crucial component to the empire. Cannabis formed the sails and ropes that led empires to colonize faraway lands. And it should come as no surprise that cannabis farming took root in those new lands, too.

When the first European colonists came to America, their sailboats were rigged with ropes made from hemp fiber. In fact, hemp was so crucial to the British navy that colonists were paid to farm it. Before the Civil War, only cotton surpassed the hemp production in the South. New Americans named their first towns for the plant, including Hempstead, New York, Hempfield, Pennsylvania, Hemphill, Kentucky, and Hemp, Georgia. George Washington and Thomas Jefferson both included hemp in their home gardens, and some claim that several drafts of the Declaration of Independence were written on hemp paper. Basically, hemp was as American as it got.

Cannabis was considered medicinal at that time, too, and it was added to the US Pharmacopeia in 1851. Low-THC cultivars were made into tinctures (see page 222) and used to treat afflictions including rabies, leprosy, alcoholism, opiate addiction, gout, insanity, and excessive menstrual bleeding.

In the early twentieth century, several factors collided to turn the tide against cannabis. Some of it had to do with racism. Carrying on an age-old tradition, Mexican laborers brought their fondness of smoking marijuana across the border as they migrated in search of a better life. Attacking weed served to demonize brown-skinned people who were willing to work for cheaper wages than white Americans. Smoking marijuana also caught on in African American jazz circles, so demonizing weed targeted both minority populations, creating a culture of fear and contempt toward the plant. Industrial pressures came into play, too, as owners of petrochemical companies invested in plastics and paper-making lobbied Congress against cannabis farming. Additionally, the temperance movement, freshly disappointed by the end of alcohol prohibition, found a new intoxicant to vilify.

By the 1930s, cannabis was essentially banned from being grown or used in the United States. The hemp industry was decimated, and mainstream society shunned the plant.

By the 1960s, though, marijuana was gaining popularity among a different subset of people who took cultivation into their own hands. Young white people traveling on the "hippie trail" returned from Morocco, Turkey, India, and Nepal, bringing experiences—and seeds—of foreign cannabis back home. Indica types—vastly different in look and high from the marijuana they'd been exposed to from Mexico—hit the scene. Foreign seeds and back-to-the-landers coalesced in Northern California, and the current epicenter of high-quality cannabis breeding and farming was founded.

Hints of purple highlights—a telltale sign of indica types in the mix of this plant's ancestry.

Northern California is the modern-day epicenter of cannabis breeding and cultivation. Here, cannabis grows amid tomatoes, zinnias, dahlias, and tall stalks of yesterday's hollyhocks. Alpenglow Farm, in southern Humboldt County, is at the forefront of sustainable cannabis cultivation, practicing regenerative farming, an approach that seeks to increase biodiversity, build soil, sequester carbon, and improve local watersheds.

The Great Sativa/Indica Debate

Peruse any dispensary or seed catalog and you'll find cannabis cultivars broken down into sativa, indica, or a hybrid between the two. You'll likely be presented with percentages of each. This is oversimplified at best, and wildly inaccurate at worst.

Centuries of hybridizing have rendered pretty much every plant a mutt between sativa and indica types. A plant's height or leaf shape isn't a reliable metric for identifying its heritage.

At this point, sativa and indica are best thought of as common names (versus botanical names) to describe the flavor of high rather than actual plant differences. Sativas refer to cultivars that are uplifting and activating, while indicas are known to be more sedative.

Are the terms *sativa* and *indica* going away anytime soon? Not likely. And it's totally fine for you to ask for cerebral/sativa highs and sedative/indica highs, but just know that a plant's actual effects are more likely due to how its unique fingerprint of cannabinoids and terpenes interacts with your own personal biochemistry. For more on the chemical makeup of cannabis, see pages 41–45.

As the tide shifts once again, we're slowly starting to embrace cannabis and all of its uses, from beauty products to pain management to—yes—getting high. Prohibition has caused immeasurable damage, namely the locking up of a disproportionate amount of people of color due to nonviolent drug offenses. We also have an agricultural crop that is eighty years behind its counterparts in terms of modern breeding and research. Our relationship with cannabis isn't new, but in many ways, it's just beginning.

Sativa types reach for that endless sun, growing taller with narrower leaflets. Their effects are uplifting and cerebral.

The Plant

Chapter 2

Weed doesn't look like anything you've ever grown before because it's not.

If you've never gardened, cannabis makes an ideal gateway crop for your foray into the soil. It grows remarkably quickly, making it super rewarding to have out back. The leaves, cultural icons in themselves, make for stunning greenery in the growing season. When it flowers, cannabis morphs from a gorgeous foliage plant into tall stalks of clustered buds that grow smellier and stickier by the day. By the time harvest closes in, the plant looks spidery and more oddball than beautiful. The leaves, the smell, the sticky flowers—it's like nothing else I've grown, and as such, it's worth having a basic understanding of the plant's anatomy and makeup.

Anatomy

Flowers

Female flowers, referred to as colas, are what you'll eventually harvest, dry, smoke, or otherwise ingest. The tight clusters are home to the highest concentration of cannabinoids and terpenes (see page 41), housed in crystal-like resin glands, called trichomes. Trichomes line all parts of the flowers, including calyxes (containing reproductive material), pistils (tiny hairs poised to collect pollen from any nearby males), and sugar leaves. Because they have less trichome density, sugar leaves

The basic anatomy of a female cannabis plant.

will be cut off after harvest, but are often saved and known as "trim," suitable for using in tinctures and other extractions (see page 222).

We'll touch on males—and why you probably don't want any in your garden—in the next chapter.

Fan leaves

Large fan leaves connect directly to cannabis stalks and do the majority of the breathing for the plant. They're the classically recognizable pot leaves, and damn, do they look good on a growing plant. Fan leaves contains some trichomes, but much fewer than on the flowers, meaning they're not part of your eventual harvest.

Stalks and stems

Stalks and stems provide crucial nutrient pathways while the plant grows. They're also the main support system for colas, and different pruning methods encourage more or less branching and flower formation.

Cannabis flowers, dried and cured.

Chemical Makeup

You grow tomatoes for the fruit, basil for the leaves, and cannabis for the chemical compounds. Here are the basics on what makes this plant so attractive to people.

Cannabinoids

Cannabinoids are the chemical compounds in pot that get you high, though they have many other nonpsychoactive effects, such as lowering inflammation or stimulating appetite. I'm certain you've heard of one cannabinoid in particular, THC (tetrahydrocannabinol), which is responsible for pot's psychoactive effects. You've also probably heard of CBD (cannabidiol), famed for quelling seizures in children without any psychoactive effects (see page 42). In fact, researchers have identified upward of one hundred distinct cannabinoids in cannabis. Some are psychoactive; others aren't. Some are found in raw cannabis plants, while others must be *decarboxylated* (heated up to remove carbon dioxide) to release their magic and have their desired effect.

We have receptors for cannabinoids all over our bodies in what's known as our endocannabinoid system. It turns out that every type of creature on earth, besides insects, has an endocannabinoid system. Humans' endocannabinoid system has a key role in appetite regulation, our ability to forget (an unsung benefit for surviving life), reducing stress, and fine motor skills. When we smoke or ingest cannabis, the cannabinoids reach the endocannabinoid receptors in our brain and nervous system and cause various effects.

Research has a long way to go on how cannabis affects our brain chemistry. Current science refers to the "entourage effect," the idea that each cannabinoid and terpene impacts another, creating highly nuanced experiences for different body chemistries. But basically, this just means that we don't know how it all works. So far, scientists can reproduce individual cannabinoids, but with actual flowers, it seems that the sum is much greater than the individual parts.

Terpenes

Adding to the unique profile of a cannabis plant is its terpene makeup. Not a term exclusive to cannabis, terpenes are chemical compounds—basically aroma molecules—that make plants smell and taste the way they do. Terpenes are found in all sorts of fruits, herbs, and plants; it's thought that they produce terpenes to fend off predators. When eaten or used by humans, terpenes have their own host

What's the Deal with CBD?

Unless you've been living with your head under a rock, you've likely heard of cannabidiol, or CBD. CBD is a nonintoxicating cannabinoid (see page 41) found in cannabis. While there are upward of one hundred cannabinoids, THC and CBD are the two most prominent. The first gets you high and the second one doesn't. These days, you can find CBD-infused oil, gummies, face masks, coffee, ice cream, eye serums, and dog treats. Its proponents swear it treats everything from acne to anxiety to autoimmune diseases to cancer. All the benefits of cannabis without the high? It's no wonder that CBD is a desirable entry point for many people who are canna-curious.

But on the other side of that curiosity and the search for a magic bullet to calm our ails are unproven claims, a scarily unregulated market, and a nonetheless exploding industry.

That's not to say that CBD doesn't have great medicinal potential. It most certainly does: In 2018, the FDA approved Epidiolex, the first CBD-derived medicine used to treat two seizure disorders in children. And currently, studies are under way to determine CBD's efficacy in treating PTSD, schizophrenia, and chronic pain. The compound is being studied for its antioxidant, anti-inflammatory, anticonvulsant, antidepressant, antipsychotic, antitumoral, and neuroprotective qualities. CBD has a lot of promise. And you probably know a number of people who swear by its efficacy, be it for anxiety or sleep.

But at this point, there are far more unknowns than knowns, and that's especially evident in the readily available, unregulated space of CBD-infused products claiming to have therapeutic benefits. Recent tests have shown that the *majority* of CBD-infused products aren't accurate in their ingredients. Some have but trace amounts of the cannabinoids they're claiming to, and some were found to contain THC, despite saying they didn't. That'd likely be an unwelcome experience to someone not expecting it.

Starting doses are a guessing game. Everyone is basically shooting from the hip with any recommendations. My husband swears by 3-mg sublingual tablets as an effective replacement for Xanax, whereas I feel nothing from them. The dosages used in clinical trials to treat anxiety are in the hundreds of milligrams, making my husband's claims likely attributable to the placebo effect. (He's fine with that. "The placebo effect is scientifically validated," he says.)

With store-bought products all over the map in terms of quality and consistency, there's all the more reason to grow your own CBD-rich cultivar of cannabis to see for yourself what therapeutic effects it might have. Cultivars high in CBD include ACDC, Canna-Tsu, Remedy CBD, Ringo's Gift, and Sour Tsunami. After harvest, you can smoke it, make a tincture (see page 222), or infuse an oil. Because there are no safe or inexpensive ways to extract just the CBD molecules at home, you'll be consuming CBD along with any other impactful properties of the plant, including THC, which varies in amount from cultivar to cultivar. This "whole flower" approach isn't a bad thing. In fact, it's fantastic. Early findings point to an "entourage effect," the idea that the cannabinoids and terpenes play off one another in a the-sum-is-greater-than-its-parts type of way. That's something that clinical trials of an isolated compound will never replicate.

"Breeder's nose" refers to the dark brown sticky spot of resin that collects on the tip of your schnoz after shoving it in enough cannabis flowers. It's a familiar condition to breeders, as terpenes, or aroma molecules, give each cultivar its individual je ne sais quoi. I'm no breeder, but I certainly find my nose brown after enough time in the garden. For me, the fragrances are the best part of cannabis gardening.

of therapeutic benefits, ranging from anti-inflammatory properties to calming ones. Usually a plant type will have a fairly narrow terpene profile. Take citrus: An orange might smell sweeter than a lemon, but both smell predominantly of citrus. Ditto for rose cultivars, pine trees, and really any plant with fragrance.

What's cool about weed is that more than two hundred terpenes have been identified, and basically, cannabis can give you all the smells—gas-like, fruity, woodsy, citrusy, floral, fruity, and spicy. But before you go on the hunt for strawberry-smelling weed, I will say this: To me, any cultivar always smells of some amalgamation of terpenes plus weed. Weed always smells like weed.

If you're like me—more gardener than smoker—terpenes might be the thing that sells you on the plant. That's absolutely what's happened in my case: I kept an arm's distance from a cannabis obsession until nearing harvest time. The flowers get so wonderfully stinky, coated with resinous terpenes, that it's hard to stay away.

Selecting Cultivars

If you're an experienced gardener, you're used to opening a seed catalog and ogling over pictures of what you might include in the garden in the coming season. Descriptions only heighten your interest, promising certain flavors, scents, or growth habits. And you can always rely on solid grow information—when, how, and where to plant, plus how tall and wide things will grow. Even if you've not done this before, it's not hard to imagine how this might be a fun activity—wheedling down colors and flavors, your mouth watering all the while.

When it comes to cannabis, the seed selection process is entirely different. Simply put, there's no two-buck seed packet with one hundred words of instructions. Catalogs of useful grow information are nonexistent. And forget seeing any photos of the plant as it grows. If there are pictures, they're close-ups of the bud, most likely shot in indoor gardens. If there is information, it's about the flavor of the high. And brace yourself: There are thousands of varieties of pot. It's daunting to the point of not being fun, especially when you don't have the useful information you really need.

Why such a difference from any other garden crop? Pretty much anything else you could ever dream of growing in your garden has gone through a modern breeding program. The process involves breeders selecting the most desirable

Strain Refrain

Though it's status quo to refer to cannabis cultivars as *strains*, that's not the correct word. Strains refer to bacteria, not plants. The proper term for all those crazy-named types of pot that someone bred is *cultivar*. It means *cultivated variety* and is used to describe a plant that's been selected and improved upon by humans through breeding. A cultivar can be a hybrid creation or a plant selected from the wild and brought under cultivation. Either way, it involves a human touch. "Varieties," on the other hand, are discovered in nature and not the result of breeding. They are plants that differ in a significant way (think: flower color) from the rest of the species. Gardeners often use *cultivar* and *variety* interchangeably—I'm super guilty of that—but the correct term for all these named weed "strains" is *cultivars*. Like *sativa* and *indica*, the term *strain* is also not likely to disappear anytime soon, but hey, why not try?

traits; one result is that the subsequent offerings shrink. Because of prohibition, cannabis has thus far avoided this fate and has really only been bred in basements. Think of it as the ultimate crowdsourced crop.

Sadly, all of that underground breeding has really focused on just one goal—maximizing THC levels, that is—creating cultivars that will get you as high as possible. Reading up on what cannabis cultivars you might grow offers little more than the supposed type of high. What that means for a gardener is that it's nearly impossible to find those other details—say, how tall something might get or what microclimate it might enjoy. Those things just haven't been tracked or considered as closely.

Hopefully that will change. Consider that during alcohol prohibition, people favored moonshine. It transported easily and got you messed up. Now that we don't have to get drunk at the risk of criminality, we can enjoy drinking a glass of pinot gris on a blanket in the sunshine. Blown-out THC levels are really just the tip of the iceberg when it comes to cannabis's potential. We are just starting to see pot bred to prioritize therapeutic effects. I'm personally excited for more aesthetic garden cultivars, say, extra-compact cultivars with variegated leaves. Additionally, there is room for improvement in regard to breeding for disease resistance. And hopefully with improved breeding and documentation will come much more accurate cultivar descriptions.

Choose based on climate?

Climatically speaking, it makes more sense to grow sativa types, which originated in the tropics, in warmer regions with longer growing seasons, as they have ample time to "finish" their extended flowering and ripening window without any chance of frost. Regions with shorter seasons are more suitable for indica types, which are adapted to higher-elevation, colder parts of the world. But as discussed on page 33, rampant hybridization has rendered true designations of sativas and indicas largely unavailable. The cultivar you choose will likely be a mix of the two, which, honestly, is great. You'll be able to get the best of both worlds without having to worry too much.

Choose based on promised high?

So, if you can't rely on selecting between indica and sativa to guide you in plant habit, can you trust them when it comes to the high? Generally speaking, maybe a little. You can usually expect that sativa types will be activating and indica types will be sedating. But again, a few words of caution: Hybridization makes those delineations imprecise. Never trust listed "percentages" of indica and sativa. They're completely fabricated. Also remember that any type of high results in a yet-to-be-understood entourage effect from the cannabinoids and terpenes that interact with your body—it's not just the amount of THC. I also really caution you against placing too much stock in the description of the high. They're outrageous, and to me clearly written by people who are stoned out of their minds. My favorite to date might be: "Smells like your grandma's house yet makes you inexplicably horny." How can this possibly be a result one can promise? Highs are subjective to one's individual brain chemistry. Personally, I've found any amount of THC to be activating, no matter how much it promises to glue me to a couch. I'm really pretty one-note when it comes to pot—I just want to clean my closet. While dancing.

Follow your nose

Until cannabis is bred for aesthetic beauty (which is something I'd care about more than the high), I recommend choosing based on bud fragrance. As a non-stoner, I'm most excited by terpenes, the essential oils of weed. Like planting a collection of different mints or scented geraniums, you might approach pot in this way: What novel smells would you like to enjoy wafting from your garden? I'm a fruit fan—cultivars promising blueberry, mango, or banana notes call my name. You might find you're a fan of pine, citrus, mint, or gasoline—all found within the terpene profiles of different cultivars.

following
Pink Lotus and Remedy CBD are two cultivars with bright pistils, pink and white, respectively, that stand out sharply from foliage when flowering begins.

Plant a diversity of colors

Many cultivars of cannabis change colors when autumn arrives, and they reach the end of their life cycle.

Pay attention to cultivar names for clues about which plants will express unique colors. While all cannabis starts out nice and green, flowering is where the fun happens with coloration. Sometimes the color happens at the start of flowering, when plants shoot out bright pistils like little puffballs of pink or lime green. They'll hold this color for several months, until they turn brown—a sign of ripening (see page 175). As flowers get bigger, the concentration of those colorful pistils gives the plant a greater punch of pink, purple, or lime green. The leaves of some cultivars really color up toward the end of the season, as light naturally diminishes and temperatures dip; some appear much like a tree in the full swing of an autumnal color change, filled with foliage in shades of burgundy, orange, and dark purple. In addition to cultivars with colors in the names, it's fair to say that a cultivar has to have some amount of indica heritage for the autumnal effects. Indicas also express more purples than sativas.

Also keep in mind that, similar to how purple string beans turn green as soon as they're cooked, the fun will be in the garden, while the plant lives and grows. Pink or lime-green pistils eventually turn amber and dry; fun-colored leaves eventually die or are trimmed away. Finished, dried cannabis buds always look a little turd-like, no matter how colorful they were in the garden. Being able to enjoy these beautiful colors is another reason to grow your own cannabis and experience the complete life cycle of the plant.

Judge them by their names

I give you my full permission to choose cultivars based on how you feel about their names. As an organic gardener, I can't really stomach the idea of cultivating cultivars like Chem Dog, Green Crack, or Chernobyl, but hey—to each their own. There are some fun names out there that seem particularly garden-friendly: Pineapple Upside Down Cake, Dirty Girl, Mango Tree, Tangerine Dream. Right? Those belong in the garden.

Try a classic . . .

There are certain cultivars that you might have heard of from Cheech and Chong movies, Hunter S. Thompson books, or your older brother, the stoner: Acapulco Gold, Northern Lights, OG Kush, Pineapple Express, Sour Diesel, and White Widow come to mind.

. . . but understand the lack of genetic accountability . . .

Here's the thing about those cult classics, though, or really any cultivar: At this juncture in cannabis history, there's little to no accountability with cultivar names. Parental lineage is more folklore than factual. And the cultivar names? Nearly meaningless. This means that one seller's OG Kush seeds might produce very different plants from another's selection. The same is absolutely true of bud you buy at a dispensary. It's actually pretty crazy—can you imagine buying two

As its name suggests, Amethyst sports dark purple foliage by the time harvest approaches.

apples labeled Fuji and having them taste entirely different? No way! But cannabis isn't there yet. We're coming out of a wonky world of underground breeding and production, with very little oversight on consistency. With genotypic mapping now available, we stand at the cusp of a much more organized world when it comes to cannabis cultivars. For better or worse, this mapping and accountability also stand to open cannabis up to the world of intellectual property rights.

... and understand the impact of terroir and phenotypic variation

Two plants with the exact same genetics *still* might produce varied cannabinoid and terpene profiles based on the *terroir* (fancy speak for soil plus climate) of their growing grounds. In fact, farmers in the three counties of California's famed Emerald Triangle (Humboldt, Mendocino, and Trinity) seek to establish appellation designations. Similar to the vintners of Bordeaux, Champagne, Chianti, and Napa, cannabis farmers are so certain of the impact of terroir on their crops that they want it certified.

Even within the exact same conditions and exact same genetics, cannabis plants still often express *phenotypic variation*, in terms of size, color, and growth. This is because a *genotype*, or genetic code, is not written in stone. Just like with humans, it defines a certain range of possibilities. The environment—water, light, soil, pests—will activate certain parts of that genetic code, resulting in a unique *phenotype*, or physical expression.

Or, don't sweat it

You're experimenting. Frankly, so is everyone else. Don't put too much stock into seed sellers' lists of easy, medium, or hard, or better for indoors or out. With legality sweeping the land, we're really at the beginning of any reliable cultivation recommendations. This is the Wild West. Shut your eyes and choose from the list at the dispensary. Learn from this season and refine your tastes for the next. Besides, if things go wrong, you can just blame the weather and try again. That's what I always do. And by the way, that's actually the real definition of a gardener: someone who kills everything *and tries again.*

Grower Profiles

Chapter 3

On his southern Humboldt County farm, Huckleberry Hill, Johnny Casali grows cannabis in raised beds amid the rest of the summer veggies, including string beans, squash, herbs like basil and cilantro, and flowers, such as marigolds and petunias.

Now let's meet some experienced cannabis growers. Far from being the typical stoners you might imagine, the farmers and gardeners who cultivate cannabis at home have varied approaches to how and why they grow, and they're all shining examples of growing weed in the garden.

The Second-Generation Grower

Johnny Casali inherited the craft of cannabis growing from his mom. She moved him from Sonoma County to

Southern Humboldt County in the early seventies when he was five years old, wanting a rural lifestyle for him.

Johnny's mom grew weed because everyone grew weed. It was a way to supplement income. There weren't a lot of jobs in the country, so you had to make it how you could. People cut firewood in the winter. They fished in the summer. And they harvested weed each fall. It wasn't to get rich; it was just to survive. Growing up, Johnny thought of weed much like he thought of a zucchini—it was just another plant in his mom's garden.

Johnny grew up in the heyday of the US War on Drugs. When he was twenty-four, with no prior criminal record, he was caught growing 1,500 marijuana plants. Thirty federal agents showed up at his door with guns to his head. Convicted of two felonies, he served nearly eight years in prison.

Afterward, he returned to farming cannabis, as it's the only life he knew.

left
Johnny Casali knows only one way of life—that of a cannabis farmer. He emphasizes beauty as much as quality on his farm, the place where he grew up and continues to live today.

opposite
You'd never know by his love of old-lady flowers that Johnny is a big, burly cannabis farmer. The man loves his colorful blooms. Here, cannabis grows in the beds of his driveway, mingling with dahlias and petunias.

In another cultivation area, custom-built, 3-by-3-foot (about 1-by-1 m) redwood boxes hold cannabis plants. They're open to the ground, letting the plants' roots commingle with the native soil. Lining the pathways is locally chipped mulch that Johnny uses to suppress weeds and keep things tidy.

After his probation ended in 2008, he felt comfortable enough applying for permits, and in 2016, Johnny's farm—Huckleberry Hill—was the fourth to receive full permitting in Humboldt County.

Johnny wants his work to matter and to make a difference in the world. For better or worse, his life is forever linked to the plant. He's finding his purpose these days in being a spokesman for humanizing the farmers growing your weed. "I'm not a bad person. I've never hurt anyone," he tells me. "I want people to see who I am."

Johnny cultivates on five thousand square feet (465 square m), growing cultivars originally developed by his mother. Those who smoke it say his weed is the best in the business. For Johnny, though, his property is about much more than cannabis. It's about having healthy fruit trees and a pond full of fish. And to accentuate his cannabis plants, Johnny turns to flowers. His style veers into granny territory—I've never seen so many petunias in my life. He wants his farm to be beautiful, lush, and full of color.

He tries to do things right, too. He's got salmon-spawning tributaries on either side of his property and he farms organically, without any sediment leaking into the creeks. He's also received the only state-sanctioned Fish Friendly certification. His favorite time of year is late summer, when the cannabis ripens and the terpenes fill his property each morning. It reminds him of his childhood and of his now-deceased mom. He knows she's looking down, so proud.

Johnny isn't sure what the future holds. While the cat-and-mouse game between the DEA and farmers throughout the eighties and nineties did nothing to curb production, legality is the thing, Johnny says, that is driving people out of business. The expenses of permitting and taxation are through the roof and the profit margins are razor thin. With cannabis still federally illegal, farmers can't get loans from banks. The challenges are endless. But he's all in. He's given his life to this plant and he can't help believing that good things are in store as we all get a grip on what he's always known: It's just a plant.

Regional Perspective

Zak Powers *on* Growing *in* New York City *and* Oregon City, Oregon

To Zak Powers, who grew up on an island in rural British Columbia, it seemed like everyone he knew grew weed. It was a major cash crop for the area, and people carried on without getting busted. "I never feared its illegality like my friends in the US," Zak says. He's now a filmmaker—you should watch his series The Yard, which documents his own adventures growing and learning about weed (he's gone as far as Italy, Israel, and the North Pole). He's cultivated cannabis everywhere he's lived, including on New York City decks, in Montana, and outdoors at his current home base in Oregon City, Oregon.

Why'd you start growing?

For a long time, an ounce of gold and an ounce of weed were the same price. It was like growing gold! I never sold the weed I grew—I just gave it away. And back when weed was illegal and you gave someone a big jar of fresh, good stuff, it was a good feeling. I liked that it was so valuable. When I gave it as a gift, it had extra special meaning, and I had extra special meaning, and that's what I crave in life. I traded weed for good feelings.

Tell me about growing outdoors in New York City.

I lived at 88th Street and Central Park West in a five-story brownstone walk-up. I put a claw-foot bathtub on the deck and surrounded it with a sea of weed plants. I had as many as twenty plants in 5-gallon (20-L) pots. I thought those pots were big enough—they weren't. I loved the plants so much and I was feeding them way too much. I burned them with synthetic fertilizer. Basically, I almost killed them by being too excited and overfeeding them.

What was the hardest part about growing in NYC?

Cops! It was the early 2000s and I was in a city of eight million people. Even though no one could see our deck (which sat above a tree-covered courtyard), we were always having parties. I was always scared that someone would call the cops, they'd find the weed, and they'd take me to jail. But I was young and didn't care.

Also, there was an obnoxious amount of pests. Caterpillars, mites—I got them all. It was Pest City. I made my own sprays with hot pepper, olive oil, lemon juice, and vinegar. And baking soda. I did different recipes from different people. It was before you could go on the Internet to learn that you should just be using neem oil. So, I'd make phone calls. I got an Ed Rosenthal book out of a library and photocopied it. We passed it around and we called it the bible. It was in a red accordion folder—I still have it. That's where we got most of our information. Even growers didn't want to go around talking to other growers because everyone was so scared of getting busted. Eventually, with the bugs, I learned that they're less of a disaster and more just a pest. So there are some holes in your plant and some spots on the leaves. You can still smoke it. You can still give it away.

So now you grow completely legally in Oregon City, Oregon. What's that like?

Everywhere else, I've had an illicit plot. It was exciting, but it wasn't a sustainable pleasure. It was like a toxic type of love. Now I can grow it as a part of my backyard. It's in my garden. Instead of roses, I plant weed.

How do you choose which cultivars to grow?

I pay particular attention to seeds grown in and adapted to the Northwest. We have a wet fall, so we need a cultivar that either flowers early or is resistant to mold. I prefer a longer growing season because I like that time with the plant, so I ask for the most mold-resistant. Because of my work, I'm lucky enough to know the breeders up here. Hermetic Genetics and Yerba Buena are two of my favorite sources for seeds.

What keeps you interested in the crop?

I can't not grow this plant. I don't know why. I have to. I grow it like it's a lotus. I don't even care about the harvest—I just have to be around the flowers. I don't smoke and these days, I can barely even give it away. Tomatoes. Tomatoes would be useful. I could feed my kids. I could give them away. But I didn't start any. I did, however, start one hundred weed plants. It's an obsession that I don't have an explanation for. I find that a lot of weed growers feel the same way.

The Urbanite

Daniel Stein is an advertising guy, not a pot guy. In his decades-long career in the business, he's worked on campaigns for many well-known packaged goods companies, including Kraft Foods, Wrigley, Jameson, and Absolut. When his firm, EVB, moved from San Francisco to Oakland several years ago, cannabis hit him right in the face: His office sits across from a dispensary and above Oaksterdam, America's first cannabis college. Optically, at least, it's the center of the industry. "We found cannabis and cannabis found us," he says.

Daniel began representing various cannabis clients—Eaze, Dark Heart

Nursery, and Harborside, considered to be the largest nonprofit medical cannabis dispensary in the nation. He figured that, while representing all of these cannabis clients, he might as well give growing the plant a try.

He had no clue what he was doing. While Daniel loves working with his hands—motors and gears—he'd never gardened. And when it came to pot, he was especially clueless: "I thought you smoked the leaves," he admits.

His first season of growing, he copied what he'd seen—trying to grow at home, indoors, with a light but not much other infrastructure. Everything promptly died. But he'd caught the growing bug. The more he grew weed, the more he realized that he was indeed using his mechanics-loving brain, only this time it was focusing on nutrients and bugs. It didn't hurt that he also amassed mentors that would make any grower jealous, including the professors downstairs at Oaksterdam.

left
Let's just say Daniel Stein finds any reason he can to visit the rooftop of his downtown Oakland advertising agency.

opposite
Sour Diesel, grown in containers, dots the rooftop, adding lushness in the heart of the city. Sunflowers, lantana, and basil round out the garden, and a bistro table and chairs make sure visitors know they're welcome.

FOX
OAKL

Following a photo shoot for some educational material for Harborside on EVB's rooftop deck, Daniel found himself with a few leftover Sour Diesel clones that would have otherwise gone into the compost. But Daniel figured it was right around Mother's Day—perfect outdoor planting time—so why not give it a go on the roof? He potted the clones up, with two going into 15-gallon (60-L) grow bags and the other into half a wine barrel.

Growing in such a conspicuous location gave Daniel pause. Having come of age during the "Just Say No" Reagan years, he still felt that internalized stigma. Even though cannabis was, by then, fully legal for recreational use, he wondered what his employees would think. And his clients.

But it turned out everyone was fascinated by it. And six months later, he had three pounds (1.4 kg) of weed.

Daniel isn't much of a smoker. Living with narcolepsy, he can only consume weed really carefully and in the comfort of his home. But he gets great joy from gifting it to friends and family. His brother, a stroke survivor who lives with paralysis and pain, finds a lot of comfort from cannabis. His mom uses it for anxiety and his dad uses it for arthritic aches and pains.

Barely a consumer, Daniel is in it for the gardening. Weed has been a gateway gardening crop for him. Cucumbers and tomatoes now trellis the wire fencing on the rooftop deck, and he's constantly working on improving his methods. By the end of last year's growing season, he'd finally connected a hose to a spigot near the rooftop deck, saving him hours of watering with one watering can at a time. Next year he might even go the distance with some drip irrigation.

A tomato cage, sunk at planting time, keeps the cannabis supported. Cheery golden blooms of lantana polish the container garden.

Regional Perspective

Casey Rivero *on* Growing *in* Central Arizona

After cofounding Yerba Buena, a sun-grown cannabis farm in Oregon, Casey Rivero now works for an LED lighting manufacturer, helping cultivators learn how to use the most efficient technology indoors. He believes that both indoor and outdoor cannabis cultivation are here to stay, and both need to figure out how to use fewer and more efficient resources. Born and raised in Arizona, Casey began his love affair with cannabis in the desert.

How'd you fall in love with weed?

I grew up in Phoenix—just a little over an hour from our southern border. Cannabis was abundant. My circle of friends discovered it at an early age because of our older siblings. It was easy to get, and it always came with seeds. My friends would be bummed about the seeds, but I was always stoked. I was like, "Let's plant them!"

What were your early grows like?

I had an old high school gym locker that my dad had gotten me for all my soccer stuff. When I was maybe sixteen, I took out all the soccer gear, lined the inside with tin foil, put in a light from a fish tank, and sprouted cannabis seeds. The outside was this blue locker with a Dodgers logo, and inside was this whole other world.

I always kept a journal. Entries were something like, "Looks good today," or "Today I watered." My mom ended up finding it all one day. She told me, "Hey, I found your little experiment in your room." I figured it was over. Then she said, "But then I saw your journals. This is a science experiment for you, isn't it?" It totally was. She let me keep the plants and watched with a wary eye.

Were those early grows successful?

Not at all! I didn't have anybody I could turn to with my questions. I didn't know how to tell a male from a female. I was reading books about other plants at the library, just hoping to find some information I could apply to the cannabis seedlings. I'd ask my biology teacher random questions, trying to get information out of him about how plants grow. I tried growing some in an alley, but it was summer in Phoenix. If you weren't standing there with a watering can, they died.

But then you figured it out?

Yes. I moved up to Flagstaff for college, and in 2010, Arizona legalized medical marijuana. At that time, it was legal to grow twelve plants of your own. You could also be a caregiver for up to five patients and grow their plants, too. I had a friend with a piece of property along the Hassayampa River, a really beautiful river, and I became a caregiver.

Observing the plants was key. Every year we'd get these moths. They'd get into our flowers. They'd eat and poop and cause mold. In time, we figured out that they were super keen on certain cultivars. So we started planting those cultivars—Northern Lights #5—on the periphery of the property, along the fence, by the river, by the trees. It seemed like the moths would do their damage to those plants on the outside and leave the rest alone.

I think that the average person would get rid of the cultivar that they knew to be pest-prone. Why'd you keep it around?

Nature adapts regardless of what you do, don't you think? If we'd taken it out, I think nature would say, "OK, then I'll eat this one." If your dog digs, do you yell at it to stop or do you give your dog a place to dig? You have to make a decision: Do you work with or against nature?

What's it like growing outdoors in Arizona?

People don't realize this, but Arizona has a lot of variation in its climate, soil, and elevation. Northern Arizona is highly volcanic. Southern Arizona is more sedimentary stone. It's got more rock and sand. The center part of the state—where I grew—is a confluence of both, plus the remnants of old-growth forest. The soil is rich, and the water table is high. It's amazingly fertile. Actually, there are a lot of amazing vineyards, too. People are finding that grapes do incredibly well in that area.

What's the hardest part?

The monsoons come in July and August and they can wreak havoc on things. It's not the moisture you worry about, but that your plants might get beaten down. It's a deluge. We can also have tornados. At the last property I grew at, a tornado took two of our fences down and ran right through the garden. It was like that scene in *The Wizard of Oz*.

Any advice for a first-timer?

Understand the capabilities of the land and the environment. And also, understand your own goals and intentions. Don't force the land to do something it's not capable of. And don't force yourself to make something bigger than it needs to be, whether it's the amount you grow or the size of the plants. Giant cannabis plants are cool. They're a novelty. They're like the thousand-pound squash at the fair. But you're not actually going to eat it because it's not going to taste good.

The Herbalists

When Cyril Guthridge and Anna Petty-Guthridge had the opportunity to make their homesteading dreams come true and raise their daughters on a piece of land belonging to Cyril's family, they jumped. Moving from Morro Bay, a beach town along California's Central Coast, to Redwood Valley, an agrarian town in rural Mendocino County, allowed them to plant roots in all meanings of the phrase. As a lifelong nature lover and licensed herbalist, Anna saw in the land the opportunity to cultivate her own living apothecary. She fills beds with calendula, a fix-all for skin; ashwagandha (*Withania somnifera*), an herb used for centuries in Ayurvedic medicine; and spilanthes (*Acmella oleracea*), a Brazilian native with bright yellow and orange flowers that, when eaten, set off an electric explosion in one's mouth and are known for antiseptic, anti-inflammatory, and antifungal properties.

There was one big catch to life on the farm: It was hard to make a living with one full-time herbalist in the family. They realized they needed a subsidy, and in Mendocino County, there's really but one subsidy of choice—weed. Growing the crop deep in the forest allowed them to pay the bills while living out their off-the-grid visions, all while keeping it quiet from their girls, whom they never wanted to put in the position of lying about their parents' occupations.

After legalization, they came out of the forest, moving cultivation into the home garden and adjacent fields. They started talking openly with their daughters about the plant, and

Cyril romances Anna with a freshly plucked bouquet of *Statice* and strawflower, two long-lasting cut flowers the duo grow to beautify the farm as well as draw in beneficial insects as a means of effective organic pest control.

ultimately, what began as a subsidy morphed into a value-added product that they were really proud of.

Now Anna, who never smokes cannabis, has deepened her training in cannabis as a medicinal herb, studying with holistic healer and cannabis therapist Wendy Read of Caretakers Garden. You don't have to get stoned to get the benefits of what she considers to be an amazing plant. Anna crafts it into salves, soaps, lotions, and tinctures, along with other medicinal herbs, using them to fight inflammation and pain.

Out in the garden, Cyril geeks out hard on the plants. Horticultural experimentation is an inherited family trait. Cyril spent his childhood in Del Mar in Southern California. He surfed and played in the garden with his dad, a landscape architect who was constantly experimenting with various palm trees and tropical plants. Cyril's grandfather, for whom he's named, is revered as one of California's original soil developers, designing blends for the state's burgeoning nursery and agricultural industry after World War II. The Guthridge men like making plants grow.

Unlike so many growers around him, he keeps his plants small, believing that the smaller the plants, the more potent the terpenes and cannabinoids. Less is more, Cyril stresses. Cannabis responds to what it's given. If you want it to grow huge, feed it and it will grow. But, he says, that's not necessary or even desirable for a good crop. His method—adapted from permaculture practices—is to use nature, not chemicals, to feed the weed. "Good soil is like a good immune system," he says. He deprives his plants of water at the end of the growing season to bring out the terpenes and flavor. From a gardening perspective, it makes perfect sense: Dry-farmed tomatoes or grapes are essentially starved into flavorful perfection.

opposite
With oak trees as neighbors, cannabis plants grow in full sun on Cyril and Anna's property.

right
In addition to cannabis, Cyril and Anna experiment with herbs, flowers, and edibles. Whenever possible, each plant serves more than one purpose, a permaculture principle known as stacking functions. For example, chamomile and yarrow both attract beneficial insects while also increasing the weed's resin and oil production. Cyril believes that any plant high in terpenes, like lavender or lemon balm, increases the terpenes in cannabis. He regularly reaches for basil, clover, bachelor's buttons, hyssop, alyssum, vetch, borage, and lupine for their abilities to attract beneficial bugs.

Regional Perspective

Denise Stubbs *on* Growing *in* Plainfield, Vermont

Although Denise Stubbs currently works in mental health, cannabis legalization is allowing her to turn her attention to her other lifelong passion—cannabis. Her nursery, Vermont Hemp Nursery, hopes to supply her region with high-CBD/low-THC cultivars.

Why'd you start growing?

My dad was a smoker, so it was already around. I started smoking weed as a teen and haven't stopped. I love how it makes me feel. My dad didn't grow it, but he was a back-to-the-lander, and I was always in the garden. I actually used to hate working in the garden, but things always seem to come full circle. When I was working on organic farms in my twenties, growing all sorts of things, cannabis was a natural progression. In 1999, I got seeds from a friend who got them from an old-time Vermont grower, and went from there. I'm self-taught, so I was winging it, especially in the beginning. I have always grown to have my own stash.

Tell me about growing outdoors in Vermont.

Until recently, it was illegal! So all of my grows have been guerilla—in hidden spots I'd have to hike to. I have friends who were willing to hike several miles, but I've never been that hard-core. Because think about it—you have to hike in everything. Any soil amendments, fertilizer, water, tools. You have to lug it all out there. My patches have always been a short hike and I've never grown more than five plants in a patch.

What about that dreadful thing you have out there— I think it's called winter?

Well, first off, cannabis loves our summers. The weather is warm and it grows like crazy. And all of that snow does have its advantages—it prevents pests and diseases from overwintering, plus it actually adds nitrogen to the soil.

But yes, a hard frost can cut a season short. Winter can come in September. For that reason, it helps to know what you're growing and have a cultivar that finishes flowering on the earlier side. Cannabis can totally handle a light frost. But if a hard frost is coming, it'll ruin the cell structure of the plant and everything goes downhill. In that case, it's best to harvest early. It'll just be a buzzier type of high.

What's the biggest mishap you've had growing outside?

I've definitely had plants die from having chosen the wrong spot for them, say, not enough sun, or in an area frequented by a moose. And I've also had some trouble with botrytis if there's too much humidity at the end of the season. But the worst is walking up to your patch and finding it's all been stolen.

You've grown indoors and out. Which do you prefer?

You cannot beat growing outdoors. Indoors, you're trying to create an outdoor environment. There is so much to do. And the plants are entirely reliant on what you do for them. Outdoors, you can skip so much. Soil, sun, and rain do most of the work.

Old-School Hippie, New-School Gardener

Zero Nylin knows his way around weed. As a sound engineer and road manager during the sixties rock-and-roll scene in Northern California, he shared joints with the likes of Bob Marley (who didn't actually pass the joint), Barry White, Terry Haggerty, Quincy Jones, and Ike Turner's band. When I ask him why he started smoking pot, he says, "There were the straights and there were the hippies. Hippies smoked weed and that was that." These days, he's got other reasons, too: Pot is the only thing that distracts him from his persistent tinnitus.

He grows but two or three plants in his backyard, and he grows them big. He gets clones from his longtime friends, fellow rock-and-roller Terry Haggerty. Terry has a prized seed collection procured from his own worldwide travels. With each seed, he can recount its journey from Afghanistan or tell the specific story of who smuggled it up from Mexico. Terry is after cultivars that offer more complexity than the exorbitantly high THC levels prized by the current market. He wants to grow weed that fuels his creativity. Zero told me once that back in the day, he and his friends considered weed to be the thing keeping them connected to the psychedelic realm in between LSD trips.

Zero's weed is good. After one visit, he sent my photographer and me home with samples from last year's crop. Rachel asked nervously, "What's this

left
Zero spends a lot of time in the yard, tending to his cannabis.

opposite
Cannabis goes from lush and foliage-filled to branches lined with dense, sticky flower buds as the season progresses.

With a creek in his backyard, Zero worries about humidity in the latter part of the season, so he pulls fan leaves to increase sun exposure on his ripening buds.

going to do? Because at night I like to take my 1:1, CBD to THC . . ." She rattled on about the products she likes. Zero spun around, looked us in the eyes, and said simply, "This is going to get you high." And it did. I tested it that night (how could I not?). I felt clear and creative. And, as per usual, I did some closet reorganization and felt like a million bucks while doing it.

following (left)
Zero grows a 1969 Colombian type crossed with a mid-1970s Afghani type. A friend of his clones plants and passes them along to Zero to grow.

following (right)
Worried about late-season humidity causing powdery mildew, Zero keeps box fans aimed at the buds as they approach harvest. I've never seen anything like this, and I love the lengths he goes to in order to protect his weed.

To his credit, Zero babies his plants. He feeds them with compost tea he makes from neighborhood chicken manure. To prevent bud rot caused by the late-season moisture from the creek in his yard, Zero hauls box fans out into the garden, pointed upward at the buds.

But if you're thinking that a peace-and-love hippie automatically knows how to garden, you're wrong. While Zero's weed is amazing, he cultivates like a pot grower, not a gardener. What I mean is this: Zero learned how to grow weed from a weed person, and cannabis is the only plant Zero's ever grown. As such, he's lacking the gardening instincts that would help him understand how cannabis is just another plant in the garden.

This is slightly hilarious because Zero's home garden is out of this world, thanks to his wife, Tilly. The couple live in Tilly's childhood home, purchased by her family in the 1950s, with a garden bearing the footprints of her father, her Italian grandparents, and every other family member along the way. A plethora of plants thrive there—six types of apple trees, two varieties of persimmon, grape vines, herbs, seasonal veggies, plus novelties like twenty-four-foot-tall (7.3-m) tree dahlias that bloom through winter. These days, Tilly practices no-till gardening and focuses on building soil. Basically, their yard is Eden.

Contrast that with the plastic kiddie pools dotting the garden—the vessels Zero uses to grow his weed instead of planting cannabis straight into the ground, thinking their isolation benefits them in some way.

Look, growing in containers is a perfectly fine thing to do, especially if you don't have room or if you have subpar soil. But the soil in Zero's yard is amazing. It's rich, fast-draining, and full of organic matter. It's the stuff dreams are made of. But as a nongardener, Zero seems almost scared of the cannabis roots interacting with the soil. He explains that the kiddie pools minimize influence from the ground. I look at Tilly, who rolls her eyes, knowing what I know: Influence from their soil would be nothing but beneficial to weed. Zero might be coming around. Six years in, the kiddie pools have degraded. There are holes in the bottoms and he knows there is some commingling with the soil. Maybe, he says, maybe he'll consider planting directly into the ground. Tilly and I smile.

After harvest, the skeletons of Zero's plants remain. Resourceful gardener that she is, Tilly puts the branches to use as trellising for sweet peas and fava beans. By spring the stalks are covered, and the cover crops add nitrogen back into the soil, making it even richer for Zero, who might be brave enough to plant straight into it next year.

The Believer

Penny Barthell is a God-fearing member of the Presbyterian church, married to a data scientist and former teetotaler. There isn't a less likely candidate for a weed proselytizer, and yet, Penny preaches the cannabis gospel.

Since Penny is an avid gardener with a pint-size backyard, every plant has to earn its real estate in the garden. With room for only one rose, she grows 'Gertrude Jekyll,' unrivaled in fragrance. The lime tree pays the rent by producing fruit she puts to use every single day. She recently made room for a new favorite, white savory (*Micromeria fruticosa*), because it makes amazing tisane (a drink made by steeping fresh herbs in hot water, versus tea, which is made by steeping dried ones). It isn't needy in the garden, and goes the distance with feeding the bees. A plant has to pull its weight for Penny to let it in.

When a friend included cannabis in her garden a few years ago, she tapped Penny—known as an experienced cultivator—for some consultation. Penny, more plant person than cannabis person, was intrigued by the never-before-seen greenery. She'd tried smoking weed in her teens, but it just wasn't a part of her social scene from college onward.

Penny found herself uncertain of how to advise her friend. Unlike with anything else she'd grown, it wasn't possible to just walk into a garden store and ask for help. "There was all this mystique," she says. "I had anxiety that there were all these special rules to grow it." Once she shook the shock of the novelty of growing weed, she allowed herself to realize that it was just

following
Amid a dahlia, a lime tree, and a smattering of herbs and flowers, Penny tends to the one cannabis plant she can fit in her garden.

another plant. She fell in love with its healthy presence, resilient nature, and fresh smell. She decided to clear some room in her tiny yard to grow her own.

opposite
"My backyard is private," says Penny, "It's where I play."

In her own garden, she first grew an indica-dominant hybrid, Amethyst. The seed-grown baby took root and grew upward of eight feet (2.5 m) tall, without any food besides rich compost at the start of the season. She didn't prune it. She barely touched it. Come fall, she harvested several pounds of cannabis and got to work doing her favorite thing to do with plants: experimenting with them in the kitchen. Penny loves making tinctures—remedies made from dissolving herbs in alcohol—with goodies from her garden, and to date, it's her favorite way to consume and share her cannabis.

She's found that tinctures are also a very palatable way to share her harvest with her circle of friends who are just warming up to cannabis, like her friends from church. All around Penny's age, they're becoming all too familiar with intermittent insomnia and muscle aches, and they're inclined to reach for natural solutions instead of drugs. Penny helps them through their canna-fears, like being concerned that their children will think they're doing drugs. Cannabis's historical roots are medicinal, Penny explains to them. As her friends soften to weed, they realize it's not the worst thing their kids will encounter, and they're more open to how it can be used sensibly and how they might be able to guide their children in the same direction.

When Penny gets together with this circle to talk and pray, they always have wine and cheese. "The table is set with an enjoyable intoxicant," she says. "I think we are still learning what it means to include cannabis in a social setting that's ours. It's not the social world of the stoner or of our teens. It's really all ours." At the last meeting, she handed out four bottles of tinctures to help with sleep. Within weeks, she had requests for more.

following
Beyond healthy soil, Penny didn't baby her plant during the season. She didn't even prune it, letting it grow completely au naturel.

Regional Perspective

Fred Lutz *on* Growing *in* Denver, Colorado

Fred Lutz has done a lot of things in his life: He's been a sergeant in the military, laid tar, driven a public bus route, and run branches for the Denver Public Library. Now semiretired, he paints, fishes, travels, camps, gardens, and, yes, grows weed.

Why'd you start growing?

I started growing the legal amount of cannabis when the laws changed a few years ago. I cat-sit for my neighbor across the street and unbeknownst to me, he'd been growing weed. He didn't get rid of the males, so it was full of seeds. To him it was worthless, but I was interested in the seeds. I thought, let's grow some pot! It's legal now! I added weed to my garden because it makes a fun gift and people seem to enjoy it more than the ubiquitous zucchini.

What do you worry about the most?

Technically, in Colorado, any weed needs to be grown in a locked enclosure, either indoors or in a basement. My yard has a six-foot (1.8-m) fence and is fairly secure, but there's still some amount of risk. A few years ago, there was an assistant district attorney who decided to go after a couple growing four plants in their backyard. The couple assumed their privacy fence was enough, and they were wrong. The head DA eventually dropped the case, but not before they temporarily lost their home and went through a hell of a lot of trouble. I can't help but feel a little paranoid.

Tell me about the climate. What's it like growing in Denver?

Truth be told, I used to grow it indoors, but my wife got mad at me for stinking up the house, so I moved it outdoors. With our arid climate, bugs just don't seem to be a big deal. We worry about hail. In Colorado, a green tint to the sky means hail is coming. I keep six-foot-tall stakes in the garden. If it's a hail day, I throw a canvas tarp over the stakes to protect the cannabis.

What do you do with the harvest?

I dry them in the motorcycle shed (I'm one of the few librarians who also speaks car). The dry takes anywhere from one to four weeks, depending on humidity. Once they snap, they're ready to trim. I put the flowers into eight half-gallon Ball jars. And I'll put them in smaller ones around Christmas when it's time to give them away. I don't smoke. I cook canna-butter and make brownies. Once every two or three months, I'll eat a brownie. I have too much to do to be stoned. But my relatives and friends love my Christmas presents. I have two friends with MS who find my weed to be a helpful aid.

How do you choose what cultivars to grow?

I inherited seeds from my neighbor and that's what I grow. I know that some weed grows tall and others grow bushy. Mine seems to be both. I have no idea what the cultivar is. My nieces call it Uncle Ed's Dank Basement weed. It's not very potent. For me, that's an upside. Apparently kids these days go for the most powerful stuff they can find, and they end up sitting on the couch for four hours. Mine doesn't do that.

Chapter 4

Seeds: *Choosing, Getting, and Starting*

Just-germinated cannabis. The rounded embryonic leaves are known as cotyledons. The ones with serrated edges are called the first true leaves.

There are two things in life that come close to convincing me of the existence of some higher power. The first is building a compost pile and witnessing the transformation of kitchen scraps and leaf litter back into delicious soil. The second is starting something, anything, from seed. It seems nothing short of supernatural that something so small can be buried and watered and will sprout a green shoot that's so full of hope just a week or so later. It's magical no matter how many times I do it.

But for a lot of people—even gardeners—starting seeds is terrifying, as though the mystery of it is enough to ensure that it won't work. This couldn't be further from the truth. So long as you can commit to keeping the soil moist through germination (as in, don't go on vacation the day after you put seeds in the ground), you're good. I promise. It really is that easy.

When it comes to starting cannabis seeds, people will try to convince you that it's complicated. They'll say you need grow lights, heating pads, purified water, or special grow mediums. None of this is true. Zip, zilch, nada. It's yet another relic of prohibition's past, which forced cannabis into closets—literally—and resulted in the need for a lot of equipment to make an indoor garden.

Why Start from Seed?

In addition to the potentially spiritual experience of witnessing germination, seeds offer the benefit of forgiveness, a taproot, and an overall less finicky, stronger plant. As juveniles, they're tolerant of a bit of tough love or less-than-ideal conditions. They can hang out in a windowsill for a while before going outdoors. This differs greatly from clones, which are replicas of older plants and exhibit less wiggle room with subpar conditions. Weed started from seed forms a taproot, one strong anchor that makes for the most efficient, effective transfer of nutrients from soil to plant. Whereas clones—rooted cuttings from mature plants—have no taproot, but instead have webs of feeder roots. Plants started from seed are just generally more vigorous and healthier than those started from clones. Be brave! Start from seed!

Expecting the Unexpected

Normally, when you buy seeds for your garden, you can expect the seeds to be stabilized and reliable, meaning you'll get essentially the same result from every single one. The result of stable seeds takes generations of breeding, crossing the parents, and then essentially inbreeding the offspring until the results are consistently homozygous.

This level of stability doesn't yet exist in cannabis. This is largely because prohibition prevented modern-day breeding programs—with their rigor and precision—from being a top priority. The focus in cannabis farming has been to breed with abandon, trying to land on some new cultivar with an insanely high amount of THC that might sweep the market and garner an award for novelty—forget stability. Furthermore, why would people keep detailed notes of breeding when it could just be adding to a jail sentence should they be busted?

At first, I found this level of instability shocking, mostly because it's just so very different from any other type of garden seeds I could buy. But I've come around to being somewhat excited by the prospect of seedlings being a bit different from one another. I'm not alone; many people view this diversity within a seed pack as a feature, not a bug. The plants might express something yet unseen—which could totally be your ticket to getting rich. In my case, it's given me the feeling of having an extra special relationship with each weed

Healthy cannabis seeds are marbled brown and should feel hard when squeezed.

baby I start from seed. I'm not looking to get rich or even sell my weed, but I like getting to know my plants and nurturing them into whomever they want to be. FYI, commercial farmers usually grow from clones because they need to know exactly what they're getting to ensure its eventual sale.

Feminized Versus Regular

Another unique-to-pot part of seed selection is choosing between regular or feminized seeds. Cannabis is dioecious, meaning there are separate male and female plants. This is pretty rare in the plant world and even rarer in the edible plant realm. Other dioecious edibles include asparagus, dates, kiwi, mulberries, persimmon, and spinach. That's about it. Except for spinach, that list is entirely vines, trees, or perennials, not quick annuals like cannabis. Also, with all of them besides spinach (which you harvest before it flowers), you need both sexes to get the fruit. Not so with cannabis. You actually only want the females. The finished buds that you smoke or otherwise use are unpollinated female flowers. If they're pollinated (by wind, as is the case with cannabis), your crop will have seeds.

Seedless pot, known as *sinsemilla* (derived from the Spanish for "without seeds"), showed up in America in the seventies. There's debate about the origin of the technique, but the practice of removing male seedlings and growing a crop of exclusively unpollinated female flowers—and thus no seeds—revolutionized cultivation in the United States. By the 1960s, seed-free weed was the hallmark of domestic production.

Beyond seeds being totally passé and a nuisance to fish out of the finished product, there's some thought that yield and potency might also diminish with males in the mix. One reason might be that the female plant makes all those powerful cannabinoids and pungent terpenes to protect herself from pests. Once fertilized, her focus is to make sure those seeds reach maturity and she has less energy for cannabinoid and terpene production.

To ensure a female-only crop, you've got two options: learn to sex plants, or buy feminized seeds.

To feminize seeds, you must stress a female plant into becoming hermaphroditic by treating it with colloidal silver or a hormone. Then, with female pollen and female flowers, all offspring from that plant are also female.

Something about feminized seeds—the language, the chemicals—is all a turnoff to me. There's also some thought that feminized seeds have less vigor and

Cannabis sex tests require ripping a small piece of the embryonic, rounded cotyledon leaf, macerating it, and mailing it to a lab.

yield than regular seeds. So, I opt for regular seeds and I encourage you to do so as well. It'll bring you more up close and personal with your plants. You'll get to learn to tell the difference between sexes, a process known as *plant sexing*, and that's language I like better.

Cannabis plants reveal their sex when they flower (something we'll cover in chapter 6, page 123). But there is a shortcut.

There's another method to sexing plants that can be done just days after germination, saving water and resources that you'd spend on unneeded male plants. Having said that, this method costs money. There are a few companies that offer sex testing. A Portland, Oregon, company, Phylos, has the most user-friendly sex tests for small-scale backyard growers. A set of four tests runs just under $60. It's not cheap, but it can be worth it if you're (a) deathly afraid of males (you shouldn't be, I promise), or (b) hell-bent on feeling like a scientist (the tests are fun to complete).

The sex test instructions are simple: After seeds sprout, the first leaves that show up are called cotyledon leaves. Every seed sprouts them—they're those rounded little leaves that emerge before the plant's first "true" leaves, as they're known. Using tweezers, rip a small part of the cotyledon off (this does no damage) and smash it onto special filter paper. You can use a pestle or the handle of a screwdriver. You mail the samples to the lab, and in forty-eight hours you'll get your results—male, female, or male* (which essentially means something went wrong and you should probably toss the plant or watch it very closely). Here's the coolest part: Cotyledon leaves are the only part of the plant with no THC whatsoever and the entire process was designed to comply with the federal Controlled Substances Act, meaning, you're not mailing THC across state lines.

Auto-flowering Cultivars

You might also be presented with the choice to buy auto-flowering varieties. While nearly all cannabis cultivars are photosensitive, meaning they take their cue to start flowering from a decrease in sunlight, some varieties have adapted to flower independently of light. Auto-flowering can be a really desirable trait for commercial, indoor growers who want a very quick crop to get to market so that they can get another crop up and running. I encourage you to embrace the photosensitive nature of most cannabis varieties and skip the auto-flowering types.

Getting Seeds

A plastic tube filled with carefully counted seeds is standard cannabis seed packaging.

The only legal way to get seeds is from a dispensary. You'll be limited to the selections they carry, which, with the overwhelming diversity that's out there, is almost a blessing. If you want to delve into all that diversity, the less-than-legal way to procure seeds is online, where seeds are sold as souvenirs. But you didn't hear that from me.

Be braced for price. While tomato seeds might cost $4 for ten seeds, you can expect to shell out $100 for ten cannabis seeds, whether you get them online or at dispensary. Why so expensive? In a phrase: a history of prohibition. When illegal, breeding cannabis plants and selling seeds assumed a great risk—hence, their great value. While this seems like a shockingly expensive price to pay for seeds, it's important to remember that growing your own cannabis is still markedly cheaper than anything you could buy, legal or illegal. A super conservative estimate of what a single cannabis plant will produce outdoors is 7 ounces (200 g). In a shop, that would cost you $1,400, before paying any crazy taxes. Suddenly that $10 per seed doesn't seem so steep, does it?

Support a Regional Seed Company

Look, I am not here to knock any cannabis breeders or the state of the cannabis industry. Actually, we all owe a major hat tip to the people who worked hard to shepherd genetics during the last one hundred years or so of prohibition. Anyone growing or breeding cannabis during that time was assuming a hefty amount of risk, while keeping the important work of cannabis diversification alive. We owe a lot to these people.

But here's the thing: Really, really good breeding is pretty scientific. It's nerdy. It's tedious. It takes attention to detail, years of perfection, and consummate record-keeping.

Getting a stable cultivar from seed takes a minimum of three or four generations of breeding, and more likely up to ten for all the seeds to pop out consistently identical offspring. Breeding is a full-time job.

Until seeds are able to be sold across state lines, your only legal option is purchasing from seed companies within your state, who sell at a dispensary. Even if this regulation changes, I still encourage you to buy from a seed company in your region, particularly one that grows their plants outdoors. Over the course of a few

left
Soaking seeds for twenty-four hours can jump-start germination. Whatever you do, label, label, label.

opposite
Sprouting seeds in wet paper towel reveals a seed's viability without having to wait to see what pops through the soil.

generations, plants adapt to their climate, making regional varieties even more prone to success in your yard. Another indicator of a solid seed company is that they genetically test their cultivars and make that information available, on either their website or their packaging.

The Nitty-Gritty—Starting Seeds

- For an optimal outdoor grow, start seeds in the late winter or early spring, depending on where you live. The timing of cannabis cultivation mirrors tomatoes. A great resource on timing your seeds is *The Old Farmer's Almanac* (almanac.com). Enter your location and you'll find the dates for starting tomato seeds and also for the best time to transplant those seedlings into the ground. Apply those to cannabis and you're set. Mark your calendar so you don't forget.
- *Optional* Soak seeds in water for twenty-four hours before planting. Do this to speed things up if you're excited, but skip this step if you're apt to forget about the soaking seeds, as they can rot if left in water too long. Soaking them in a little glass jar on the windowsill is perfect.
- Pot seeds into 4-inch (10-cm) or gallon-size (4-L) containers filled with fresh potting soil. A good rule of thumb that translates to all seeds is to bury them twice as deep as the seed is wide.

RY MUFFIN
ANGO TREES
OG KUSH

- Windowsills are OK for a few weeks, but full sun and fresh air are the most conducive to healthy growth.
- Keep the soil moist throughout germination. This isn't rocket science: Just shower them with water once a day, less if the weather is cold and the soil is staying wet.
- If possible, make conditions a little warmer and safer for the seedlings. You can buy a product called floating row cover—white fabric that lets in water and light and adds a little insulation—to do the job. Or you can cut the bottoms off plastic milk jugs to create homemade cloches, or mini greenhouses. I splurged and bought myself a $30 greenhouse on Amazon (see page 242). Keeping seeds covered also ensures that birds, slugs, and any other small creatures will leave them alone.
- Seedlings are ready to be planted directly into the ground or their containers in early summer. Again, refer to *The Old Farmer's Almanac* and reference tomato transplanting for your location. For more on how to transplant your seedlings, see page 142.

opposite
Starting seeds in small containers helps you keep track of what's what. Also, using movable containers allows you to rotate them and keep them in full sun. For example, my seedlings' eventual home in a raised bed doesn't get full sun until early summer.

right
My babies hung out in a waist-high, zippered plastic greenhouse, giving them a little extra heat and protection from the elements in those early days.

Chapter 5

Clones: *What They Are, Plus Pitfalls and Opportunities*

While a clone might look like a baby, it's not actually juvenile. The vegetative cutting is an exact genetic replica of its mother plant.

If I've still not sold you on starting from seed, your other option is to purchase a clone—a living plant—from a dispensary.

If you've ever grown anything else in a veggie or herb garden, you know you can choose between starting from seed or grabbing a seedling at the nursery. You start from seed if you're prepared, and you grab seedlings if you've waited too long. A veggie seedling is simply a seed that someone else has started for you at the right time of year.

With cannabis, you have the choice of starting seeds or procuring a clone. While this may seem like the age-old seed-versus-seedling conundrum, it is so not.

A clone is not a seedling. As the name implies, a clone is an exact copy of its mother plant. It's what we'd call a *vegetative cutting* in non-cannabis horticulture. But again, prohibition and all that in-the-basement breeding led to cannabis having its own horticultural lingo. In this sense, cannabis clones are closer to what you're grabbing at the nursery when you reach for an ornamental plant. Whether annual or perennial, from mums to salvia to gaudy petunias, nearly all are vegetative cuttings that have been taken from a mother, rooted, and grown. They're clones.

A cannabis clone guarantees you a few things. First, you know you're getting a female—which is important, as we've discussed (see page 103), for ensuring a seed-free crop. You can skip the plant sexing. Clones also ensure that you're getting an exact replica of a known plant. That's a big deal in the murky world of cannabis genetics. Not having gone through a modern breeding program (yet), cannabis seeds aren't yet stable and there's no guarantee that those OG Kush seeds will all turn out the same, or that they'll even resemble that OG Kush you remember from your high school stoner days (not that you know what you were actually smoking in high school).

Seems great, right? Seems like clones would be a no-brainer. But cannabis clones provide a few challenges of their own.

Plant Pathogens

Here's something you might not know about all those plants, from mums to salvia to the petunias: The ornamental horticulture industry uses tissue culture—we're talking white coats and petri dishes—to clear plants of viral loads and pathogens. Whether you grab them at a giant box store or a teeny tiny independent nursery, those rooted cuttings come from sterilized stock that's refreshed every year. Mind-blowing, I know, but that's how the industry prevents the buildup of diseases that can wipe out a crop.

Not so with cannabis—yet. While tissue culture is starting to happen at the periphery, it's still not the norm, meaning clones aren't sterilized of plant pathogens. If anything, the viral load builds from year to year, and might eventually prove disastrous. We can look to history for an example: The state of the cannabis industry right now looks a lot like ornamental horticulture did thirty years ago, before tissue culture was used. At that time, certain crops, like geraniums and New Guinea impatiens—super-common bedding flowers—were much more prone to crop failure due to a built-up viral load. Now, tissue culture ensures that the plants you buy at the nursery have been grown from sterilized stock. With cannabis, breeders and growers are still doing their own propagation from mother plants, often totally unaware of the disease issues that could ruin everything.

Light, Light, Light

You can start seeds outdoors without any lights or equipment, because seeds are young and forgiving. They're in a juvenile state that makes them resilient to less-than-perfect conditions. Clones, on the other hand, are not juvenile. They're small cuttings of fully mature plants. And being photosensitive, they're ready to snap from vegetative to flowering at a moment's notice. Indoor growers will try to freak you out about this. They're so accustomed to controlling every last element of

Mother plants grow indoors at Dark Heart Nursery in Oakland, California.

their cannabis plants' lives. They flip a switch and their plants go from vegetative to flowering (see page 155 for an explanation of these terms).

But as long as you get your clone into the ground at the right time—very late spring or very early summer—nature will take its course and you should be OK. You'll want to harden off your clone before transplanting it (see page 120).

Where to Buy Clones

Just as with seeds, the only legal place for you to buy a clone is a licensed dispensary. And again, you'll be limited to growing what cultivars they have available. There are a few important things to note. First of all, at any respectable garden store, they're only going to sell you plants that will grow at that time of year; they're not going to put out tomato starts in the middle of winter. Not so with cannabis. Because many grow operations are indoors, dispensaries sell clones

year-round. It's up to you to grab your clones at the appropriate planting time for your region. A good rule of thumb is to plant around Mother's Day, or several weeks after the chance of frost. The other thing to note is that a dispensary is not a garden store. Expect mixed results from employees when you ask them your grow questions.

Hardening Off Clones

If you're growing from a clone, it's highly likely that that little lady has been stored under twenty-four-hour artificial light for quite some time. She's going to go through a pretty massive transition moving from artificial indoor light to the outdoors. It's best to ease your plant into its new environment slowly to prevent shock. This gradual ease-in, known as hardening off, will serve you with cannabis in addition to any other crop you've grabbed from the nursery, from tomatoes to beans, that might have been in less-than-perfect conditions for a while.

First, you need to make sure that the clone is planted in a growing medium, namely fresh potting soil, that can support it for a few days without drying out every few hours. Clones are often sold in Rockwool (which is made from heating spinning rock into long fibers and traditionally used in insulation). Rockwool holds water but dries super quickly. Forget about your plant and you'll find it wilted and dead in no time.

Next, harden off your clones by slowly getting them acclimated to outdoor conditions over the course of a week. It helps to store your containers in trays, at this point, to make transporting easier. Take your clones to a protected location outside, say, on a deck, for one hour of full sun. Add one hour for each day of the process, and by the end of one week, you'll be at seven hours, aka full sun. Let's say you've got a busy life that impedes your ability to be the perfect hardening-off queen; just do the best you can. The first few days, put them out when you wake up and take them in before you leave for work. The next few days, let them hang out in the shade while you're gone, bringing them in when you get home. And for the final few days, put them in a spot that gets full sun for part of the day. You'll be fine. The goal is just some sort of transition period to minimize shock.

previous (left)
These clones are headed for dispensaries where they'll be sold. They've lived their lives completely under artificial lights, never having seen the sun. While dispensaries sell them year-round to supply indoor growers, for whom seasons don't matter, you need to plant them at the right time of year—usually early summer—for them to behave like you want them to, growing big and strong before flowering.

previous (right)
You'll likely buy your cannabis clone rooted into a medium known as Rockwool.

opposite
A few days of dappled sunlight helps harden off clones and minimize any shock when you get them into the ground.

Growing Weed

Chapter 6

You've waited long enough. Let's dig in.

Weed is a weird crop to grow. With anything else, you head to the garden store, buy the plant, and also hopefully interact with a nearby employee who knows a thing or two about growing said plant. This is not the case with cannabis. You can only buy the plant from a dispensary, which is arguably not the best place to get grow information. Dispensary employees likely know more about indoor cultivation, if any cultivation at all, and they're very likely to scare you with myths and misinformation. Additionally, the Internet is filled with resources, but many of them are completely unreliable. So far, most information on growing weed remains geared toward the indoor grower.

In the disjointed world of cannabis cultivation, how do you find your people? Look for a local hydroponic or grow shop. Yes, *hydroponic* refers to indoor cultivation, but I'm telling you:

This is where the experts work. This is where the cultivation geeks gather. They may or may not be stoners obsessed with the crop, but they are most certainly addicted to the growing. They know the local climate, the local pests. They likely deal with home-scale grows and with people who are growing for all sorts of reasons other than selling their harvest. Basically, they're the gardeners.

It helps to have people. Don't be too proud to seek out some hand-holding. As I made my way through my first growing season, I was certainly able to apply plenty of my own horticultural expertise to the endeavor, which was helpful. But with weed, you just hear so much weird information left over from prohibition days that it helps to have some experts to consult with, or in my case, provide therapy and the assurance that it will all be OK.

By the way, if you're in the Bay Area, Berkeley Indoor Garden is your spot.

THE ENZYME STRIKES BACK
TO THE FUTURE
CANNA
Vegan Mix
3-2-2
All Purpose
4-6-2
Vegetable Garden
4-4-4
Fruit Tree
6-2-4
Crab Meal
4-3-0
Shrimp Meal
Kelp Meal
Blood Meal
12-0-0
ALL NATURAL FERTILIZER
DOWN TO EARTH
CANNA
CANNA
NATURAL PLANT

opposite
A hydroponic store selling no living plants might very well be the best spot to find localized, expert advice about cannabis cultivation. Pictured here: Berkeley Indoor Garden in Berkeley, California.

They've been in business since 1984 and have endured a lot, like being shut down in 1989 by Operation Green Merchant, the DEA's effort to close shops thought to sell cannabis cultivation supplies. They're very skilled in hand-holding. But be forewarned: As nice as they are, they keep a quote wall in the back room, highlighting some of the more hilarious things they've heard from customers. "Mom, I told you to stay in the car" tops my list.

Jamal, an employee there, was the kindest soul to me during my first grow season, helping me wade through the differences between indoors and out, and why the information that farmers were telling me might not apply to my six plants out back. We talked about local weather patterns and weighed the pros and cons of harvesting before the first rainstorm of the fall. With his encouragement, I trusted my instincts to wait and give the flowers a little more time to ripen. I was able to proceed with confidence that they'd dry out after the storm. They did.

Assess Your Conditions

Don't come at me in a few months with failing plants, convinced that they have some rare soil-borne disease. I see this all the time with vegetable gardens, and in nearly every single case, the gardener just didn't give the plant what it wanted from the start. So many plant problems come from inadequate environmental

right
I drove by this shop thousands of times before ever knowing what it was. At first, I thought it sold houseplants. Then I learned it was all about growing weed, but I had no interest. Years later, it's a place I frequent regularly for supplies and advice.

No two ways about it—weed needs full sun, meaning a minimum of six hours each day.

conditions—too much or not enough sun, too much or too little water. No amount of TLC is going to make up for a sun-loving plant being shoved in the shade. Plan appropriately from the start, and Mother Nature is going to be working with you, not against you.

Find the Light

Cannabis is a sun-loving summer annual herb (I'm using the botanical meaning of *herb*: a plant without a woody stem that dies to the ground after flowering). If you've already got a veggie patch where your peppers and tomatoes thrive, this is where you plant your weed. If not, you're on the hunt for a part of your yard that gets full sun (meaning at least six hours of direct sunlight) in summer. To determine your sun exposure, assess light patterns every hour or two over the course of a full day, noting where shadows fall. Keep seasonality in mind. Bare-branched trees offer sunny spots below them in spring, but those spaces become shady in summer.

Yes, it's really that simple. All those crazy indoor situations with grow lights and complex lighting schedules vanish when you move the grow outdoors. The sunshine offers the full spectrum of light to your cannabis plants. Even better news: Because the sun moves in the sky, hitting different leaves at different times, you can also avoid all sorts of weird pruning that indoor growers have to do in order to compensate for having static lights that hang from above.

Consider Size and Spacing

How big this thing gets is variable, and actually quite in your control. You may or may not have seen crazy-tall weed plants, more aptly called weed trees. Those things have trunks! More likely than not—I mean, not unless you're planting in the original soil of the Fertile Crescent—that's not going to happen on its own. Weed trees are coaxed into that growth, either organically or not. In the world of organics, it's done with an almost daily application of compost tea.

Beyond grower influence, size is also affected by cultivar. Sativas, which are historically from equatorial regions, grow taller with wispy, narrow leaves, while indicas—from northern climates—grow smaller in stature with fatter leaves. But remember: Hybridization means you should take that information lightly.

Generally speaking, give a plant everything it wants, and it'll grow big. Compromise something—light, water, nutrients—and it'll grow smaller. Less than ideal conditions also open the door for mildew and pests. Honestly, plant your weed in full sun and you're not likely to encounter any problems.

I'm actually a big fan of purposefully not overdoing it with size. As a gardener, I know that bigger isn't always better. Dry-farmed tomatoes, stressed to near death, give everything they've got to make those fruits as tasty and concentrated as possible, whereas overfed, overwatered, overnurtured tomatoes taste like water to me.

opposite
You need to find a large enough planting space to give your weed some breathing room.

Surprise, surprise: Bigger isn't always better. The case for petite-size plants:

- **I don't need that much bud.** Turns out even one or two plants, grown without much fertilizer, will still give you *way* too much weed (at least several ounces to half a pound, or 225 g, per plant).
- **Bigger plants are harder to care for.** Between creating a proper trellising structure to having to climb a ladder to check on and harvest buds, who needs that?
- **Bigger buds are harder to dry.** Oversize colas just mean more precision and accuracy are needed when it comes to making sure the buds dry evenly from inside out. There's more chance for rot or mold to form.
- **Bigger plants draw more eyes.** I mean, maybe you don't mind. But if you're looking to keep your pot sort of inconspicuous, no need to grow monsters.
- **Bigger isn't always better.** Don't feel like a failure for not trying to grow the biggest plants. I met several Humboldt County farmers who specifically starve their plants of nutrients and water, embracing more of a dry-farming approach, similar to dry-farmed tomatoes or corn. The idea is that stress forces the plant to focus all of its energy on reproducing—aka making amazing, flavorful flowers. I've witnessed fields of weed measuring just two feet (60 cm) tall with a farmer giddy that he'd have the best-tasting buds.

I'm not trying to get you to intentionally stress, starve, or restrict your plant's growth in any way. But don't fall for the myth that bigger plants are better. The point is: Size is going to vary based on conditions and your approach as a gardener. A safe bet is to leave each plant five to six feet (1.5 to 1.8 m) in diameter and expect them to reach up to eight feet (2.5 m) tall. This gives you ample breathing room around each plant—a good idea for encouraging air circulation and minimizing problems pertaining to mold and mildew. When in doubt, give a little more room. By the way,

following (left)
Quarter-inch (6-mm) drip tubing with predrilled emitters keeps this cannabis baby watered efficiently from start to finish.

following (right)
Does it get any more on-trend than cannabis and succulents? Here weed sits pretty alongside a spineless *Agave attenuata* and multibranching *Aeonium decorum*.

What's Up with Those Felt Pots?

Cheap, lightweight felt pots are a classic cannabis-growing choice. The theory goes that the fabric "air prunes" the roots, meaning that when the roots hit the fabric, they stop growing but continue taking up nutrients. In other containers, say made of plastic or clay, the roots keep growing and the plant risks becoming root-bound, forming a mass of roots in the pot that churn through water and nutrients much faster, risking a stressed-out plant. I'm not sold on this theory; so long as your container is big enough (again, 15 gallons/60 L is ideal), you're 100 percent fine growing in any kind of container you'd like. After all, the plant isn't going to live in the long term—only one season. I worry about plants getting root-bound when they're fast-growing babies stuck in too-small pots (think about the stressed-out tomatoes at the nursery), or fruit trees that live for years and years in one container. My cannabis plants have done fine in all sorts of containers, including plastic, ceramic, and felt.

What I do like about the felt pots is that they're extremely lightweight, making them a cinch for hauling around the yard as sunlight patterns change throughout the season. They're cheap. They also store well—just fold them up and toss them in the corner. I'm not in love with their aesthetic, and I find that they quickly get stained with dirt. They're not the only lightweight option in town. Check your local nursery (or even Target or IKEA) for cute lightweight options. Drill holes if they don't have any.

right
Growers often use affordable, lightweight felt pots. Here, I've added some zinnias in smaller-size pots for added cheer. Let's just say my container plantings were a hit at my son's first birthday party.

following
Weed growing behind a secluded tall fence in a Marin County, California, garden.

this is a good rule of thumb when it comes to planting just about anything in your garden. (Except succulents—jam those together.) Again, don't feel bad if your cannabis doesn't reach eight feet tall. Some of my finest pot has come from the smallest plants.

Make Sure You're Set with Water

Easy access to irrigation is paramount. I cringe when people tell me how excited they are to garden that year and swear to me up and down that they'll be just fine carrying a few buckets from the sink inside. It just never works. If you've got a spigot, you're in luck. At the bare minimum, attach a hose with a nozzle at the end. Choose a hose that wraps easily and doesn't kink. And remember to get coverage when you leave town.

Drip Is Best

Drip systems are low-pressure, low-volume setups that deliver water exclusively where it's needed—at the root zone of the plant. Using a drip system minimizes evaporation, weeds (the non-cannabis kind), and problems related to moist conditions. Setting up a drip system is so much simpler than it sounds. Buy a kit from a local hardware or garden store and do it over the course of a few hours on a weekend. Drip systems require no special plumbing experience and no fancy tools. Snag a Y-valve from the store, allowing you to turn your faucet into two, so that you can attach a drip-irrigation system to one side and preserve the other for a regular garden hose.

Skip the Soakers

Please refrain from using porous soaker hoses that seep water along their entire length (regular garden hoses are just fine). Because of their ease of setup, soakers are often used as a shortcut to drip irrigation. Skip them for your cannabis (and, if you ask me, for all of your edible crops). Made from recycled rubber tires, they leak toxins into the soil. Cannabis is a known soil remediator, meaning plants pick up toxins from the soil (it was used to clean the soil in Ukraine after Chernobyl). It'll do all-too-masterful a job soaking up those toxins—things you don't need to ingest down the line when you enjoy your harvest.

If Needed, Acquire Containers

Containers make a great choice for a sunny balcony, poor soil, or even just because cannabis looks really pretty in a pot. Like with anything else you put in a container, you want to make sure there are drainage holes on the bottom (no, a few inches of rocks do not count as drainage, ever), and that the container is large enough to support the roots—go no smaller than 15 gallon (60 L) with weed. Make sure you have plenty of potting soil on hand at planting time. Heavier containers often benefit from being placed on plant stands or even a few bricks in order to encourage water to drain out the bottom.

Know the Rules

Luckily, legalization means I get to avoid the intimidating part of the classic weed books of yesteryear. I can refrain from telling you how to trek water through a forest, which is great, because I have no idea. But we do need to address regulations. It's important to know the laws in your locale. Educate yourself about the laws in your particular municipality by checking online. Certain areas might require that you keep your plants behind a tall, locked fence. Your local municipality also l ikely regulates the number of plants you can grow per household. Where I live, it's six—way more weed than I'd ever need in one lifetime.

At some point in your grow, things get real. For me, it was the first time I was confronted with drying and curing my plants, realizing just how smelly the project would be, and being completely unsure of where I'd set that up. Though completely legal in my state, growing weed is still federally illegal. I wasn't scared I'd go to jail, but as a renter with a lawyer for a landlord and a clause in my lease about no illegal drugs, I came face-to-face with the reality of this activity assuming some risk. A wise woman once told me to say sorry instead of asking for permission, so I persisted, praying that neither would come to pass. It's just something to consider, especially if you have a risk-averse husband like I do.

following
Here I am adding bat guano and bone meal—though, honestly, you're fine with good old-fashioned organic compost.

Prep Your Soil

As a gardener who embraces organic methods, I believe in feeding soil rather than feeding plants. This creates a healthier ecosystem on the whole. And if I'm honest,

ALL NATURAL FERTILIZER
Bat Guano
9-3-1
The undisputed champion of all natural fertilizers, our nitrogen-rich Bat Guano also provides essential phosphorus and potash for vigorous vegetative growth and prolific fruit and flower development. Bat Guano is highly effective mixed into soils, applied as a side dress or steeped to make a potent guano tea or foliar spray.
GUARANTEED ANALYSIS
TOTAL NITROGEN (N) 9.0%
2.7% Water Soluble Nitrogen
6.3% Water Insoluble Nitrogen
AVAILABLE PHOSPHATE (P_2O_5) 3.0%
SOLUBLE POTASH (K_2O) 1.0%
Derived from: Bat Guano
Product of Indonesia
Listed by the Organic Materials Review Institute (OMRI) for use in organic production.
APPLICATION RATES
8 cups ≈ 1 lb; 1 cup ≈ 2 oz; 1 tbsp ≈ 0.1 oz
Vegetable Garden & Flower Beds: To prepare new gardens, apply 1-2 lbs per 100 square feet and thoroughly mix into the top 3" of garden soil. For new transplants, add 1 tsp per hole, mix into soil and water in well. To feed established plants, side dress 1-2 tsp, depending on size of plant and desired growth rate, once each month during the growing season.
Outdoor Containers: For new plantings, add 1-2 tsp per gallon of soil and mix thoroughly OR add 2.5-5 lbs per cubic yard. To feed established plants, lightly mix 1 tsp per gallon into the soil surface once each month during the growing season.
Liquid Preparations: Add 1-2 tbsp per gallon of water and let steep up to 48 hours, agitating periodically. Apply the solution directly to the soil around plants or and apply as a foliar spray. Be sure to use all of the solution once it is prepared.
OMRI LISTED
PLEASE STORE AWAY FROM PETS
Visit us online at: downtoearthfertilizer.com
DOWN TO EARTH
ALL NATURAL FERTILIZERS
Net Wt. 25lbs., 11.3 kg.
ALL NATURAL FERTILIZER
Bone Meal
3-15-0
COMPOST THIS BOX!
DOWN TO EARTH
ALL NATURAL FERTILIZERS
OMRI LISTED
NET WT 6 LB (2.72 kg)

DOWN TO EARTH
Bat Guano
9-3-1

opposite
Dig a hole double the size of your planting container.

I'm a lazy gardener. I like to set my babies up for success and then sit back and let them show me what they can do. Luckily, organic compost and a few other choice amendments (something added to improve the soil quality or fertility) satisfy both my organic and lazy sides. Compost is decayed organic matter. It's the ultimate food for your soil, which is the ultimate food for your plants. Add plenty to your in-ground hole when you plant, and you should be good for the season. If you're planting in containers, use fresh potting soil—nothing recycled from last year. I'll discuss ongoing fertilization (which honestly is totally optional) on page 151.

If you want to get fancy, there are a few amendments that can be added to your soil that are very classically for cannabis. They are absolutely used with other garden crops, too, but the specific duo of bat guano and bone meal is favored by cannabis growers for its help in the beginning with growth, and at the end with flowering. The first, bat guano, is high in nitrogen and is perfect for those early weeks of growth. The second is bone meal, high in phosphorous, which will help your plants flower later in the season. It's OK to use both at planting time, as the bone meal takes time to become bioavailable to plants, and there's no need to add more later—you should be set for the season.

To amend your soil, use a digging fork to turn over the existing earth, breaking up clods with your hands. Then rake the area smooth. Add a 4-inch (10-cm) layer of organic compost along with any other soil amendments you're choosing to include, fork it in, and rake smooth once again. Voilà, your bed is prepped.

Get 'Em in the Ground (or Containers)

Give both your little transplant (clone or seedling) and your planting area some water before planting time. This helps to minimize shock. Dig a hole double the size of the baby and then gently sink her in, careful not to disturb any roots. As you backfill the hole, the soil line should hit the plant at the base of the stem. Water again immediately. Try not to step too close to your plant. Healthy, living soil needs oxygen, and compacting the ground is a sure bet to muck that up.

following
Slip your plant out gently. Squeeze the bottom of the container if it needs a nudge, but try not to disturb the plant's sensitive roots.

My favorite time of day for transplanting (fancy speak for planting) anything is the early evening. The soil is still warm from the day, but the worst of the heat and sun have passed. Your little plants will be able to settle in over the evening. If you're not able to do an early evening planting, aim for early morning,

as you've likely still got some cooler temps to work in your favor for a few hours. And if you really have to do the middle of the day, shoot for a cooler, overcast day, and consider a makeshift shade structure (the lid of a cardboard box propped up with a stick will do). Basically, it's best if you can ease the plant into a new home with as little extremes (sun, heat) as possible.

Lay a Security Blanket

A protective layer of mulch is almost always a good idea in a garden. It retains moisture, mitigates temperature fluctuations, and keeps weeds at bay. I avoid straw because it tends to be a snail magnet. I opt for 3 to 4 inches (7.5 to 10 cm) of finely chopped bark mulch or around the same thickness of additional compost, not forked in.

How Much to Water: The $64,000 Question

The only permissible answer to the question "How much should I water this?" is "It depends." If you're ever given any other answer, about any plant, run. Watering amount depends on weather, soil type, and how long the plant has been in the ground.

The younger the plant, the shallower the root system, which requires more frequent watering to prevent those little baby roots from drying out. As the season progresses, root systems grow larger and more robust. Most plants have as much mass underneath the soil as they do above, and they grow stronger and more resourceful, allowing you to stretch out the time between irrigations. For the first few weeks, check on your cannabis daily as it gets established.

After that, get into a rhythm based on the weather and your soil. If it's been sunny and windy, with little moisture in the air, the plants are going to dry out quickly. If you've had an overcast few days, the moisture in the soil is going to be absorbed more slowly. If you know your soil to be on the sandy side, you can plan on it drying more quickly, while you can expect clay soil to retain moisture.

Place that puppy in the ground. The soil should be level with the base of the plant.

While I can't make an irrigation schedule for you, I can offer you a simple rule: Water when the soil is dry down to about ½ inch (12 mm). Skip any fancy app or implement and just use your finger. Stick it in the soil to your first knuckle. If the soil is dry, it's time to water. This might be once a week. It might be once every several. The sweet spot is likely every three to five days. Sufficient rainfall (meaning the soil gets saturated to several inches down) counts as a watering.

With almost all of my garden plants, I prefer deep, infrequent waterings (after the period of establishment). I like to leave the drip system on long enough (fifteen-ish minutes) for water to penetrate past the root zone, encouraging roots to grow deeper. When I'm watering a container, I make sure I see water coming out the bottom before I stop.

Forget to water your plants for a few weeks, and they'll die. But similarly, don't go overboard. Overwatering puts your plants at much greater risk for rot and mildew. Let your soil dry down a bit before watering again. One rule of thumb I've always liked is to take some soil and make a ball in the palm of your hand. Throw the ball up and catch it. If it retains its shape, the soil is still wet. If it falls apart, you're ready to water.

Lastly, do what you can to keep foliage dry. Drip irrigation makes this a nonissue. If you're watering by hand, stand close to the plant and aim the spray at the soil, watering a circle of soil as wide as the plant's circumference.

Troubleshooting

So long as you plant your cannabis at the right time of year, in rich, well-draining soil, with plenty of sun and room for air circulation, and you don't overwater it, not much is going to go wrong. Problems are much more common in indoor conditions. If you're new to the garden, I encourage you to embrace the great outdoors and understand that you're sharing space with a whole lot of other living organisms, from soil microbes to insects to birds. Your garden doesn't exist in a vacuum, nor should it. Most of the time, everyone gets along well enough.

Paying a little attention goes a very long way. There's an old saying in sustainable agriculture: "The best fertilizer is the footprint of the farmer." I love this. The number one thing you can do to prevent problems is to get outside, hang with the plants, and give them a good once-over from time to time.

Having said that, let's talk about the most common problems in an outdoor grow and what to do should they arise in your garden.

Animal

Deer Whether you have to worry about deer varies based on your geography. While cannabinoids often deter herbivores, deer are the exception. Prevent problems by spraying organic repellants (look for odors of garlic, pepper, or rotten egg) or fencing.

Gophers These midsize rodents are notorious for feeding on roots and sucking entire plants underground into their tunnels. Prevent problems by planting cannabis in containers if you know gophers to be an issue in your area, or plant in raised beds lined with gopher wiring. Treat problems by trapping them. Yes, you have to then dispose of dead rodents, but it's the most effective and least toxic means.

Snails and slugs These slimy creatures favor munching on tender young leaves. They present much less of a problem as plants grow tall. Prevent problems with a sprinkling of iron phosphate (Sluggo is a brand name that has a pet-safe formula), a permissible organic treatment. Treat problems by plucking off snails and slugs by hand. Either collect them at night when they're active or place a beer-filled saucer nearby and watch them die.

Spider mites These sap-feeding arachnids collect on the underside of leaves. They're hard to see with the naked eye. Prevent problems by making sure your garden is filled with beneficial insects. The surest way to do that is to practice polyculture, explained on page 151. Treat problems by spraying organic neem oil on the undersides of leaves. You might have to do this several times. Be sure to avoid spraying flowers, as the residue can alter their flavor.

Whiteflies You'll know when you have an infestation of these sap-feeders, as any disturbance to the plant (like gently shaking it) causes a mass of tiny white bugs to take flight. Prevent and treat problems by hanging yellow sticky traps near plants. Sold at any garden store, these sticky cards attract whiteflies, greatly reducing their population.

Fungal

Gray mold (aka bud rot or botrytis) This is probably the most common fungal problem for a weed grower. It appears on flowers as a grayish film and gets fuzzier as it spreads. An outbreak of gray mold renders flowers rotten and unusable. Prevent problems by making certain plants grow in full sun and aren't overwatered. Treat problems by pruning out affected branches and disinfecting your pruners in alcohol before using them again.

Growing Weed in the Garden

Planting flowers or herbs adds cheer, draws in beneficial insects, and creates a stronger ecosystem. Here cannabis plays nicely with orange cosmos.

Powdery mildew When afflicted by this fungal problem, plants look like they've been dusted with a powder. The fungus impedes growth, and if buds even form, they won't be usable. Prevent problems by making sure your plants are in full sun and have some breathing room between them. Treat problems by spraying a solution of one teaspoon (5 g) baking soda with one gallon (4 L) of water. Check and spray daily until the outbreak is gone.

Plant Some Friends

An ecosystem is always stronger when it contains different kinds of plants growing together, a practice known as *polyculture*. Another way of saying this: Plants like friends. Flowers and herbs provide a habitat and food for beneficial organisms, like ladybugs, parasitic wasps, and green lacewings, which in turn will hopefully do their job and destroy pests who dare visit your garden. Also, flowers are pretty, and herbs smell good—what more reason do you need?

There are all sorts of theories out there about good companion plants for weed. I know a farmer who swears that growing yarrow (sweet little flowers with somewhat vigorous roots) provides just enough root competition to make weed fight for its life and thrive. I know another farmer who loves to plant smelly herbs (like chamomile and sage) nearby because he's certain that the terpenes play off of one another. There's also the farmer who plants potatoes under his pot plants (pot-tatoes, get it?) because he's certain that the potatoes attract a soil microorganism that might otherwise feed on cannabis roots. And many people plant sunflowers on the periphery of their gardens, intending to catch the bad bugs before they reach the pot plants. These are all great theories. And they're just that—theories, not absolute mandates. Plant something that brings you joy.

Go Gentle on the Food

People go really, really overboard with fertilizing their pot plants. Serious growers brew their own compost tea and *fertigate* (fertilize + irrigate) every time they water. I wholeheartedly advise against this practice, as it's a) labor intense, and b) going to make you grow much bigger plants (see my reasons against this in the size and spacing section, page 129).

Instead, take it easy. It's hard to go wrong with organic products. They decompose quickly, making it nearly impossible to harm (burn) your plants.

opposite
A repurposed tomato trellis provides the perfect amount of support for your cannabis.

In-ground, you don't need more much than good old-fashioned compost at the time of planting. If you've not got your own pile to pull from, buy the bagged stuff from your favorite independent nursery. I prefer locally sourced compost for a lower carbon footprint and the juicy reuse of local materials. Don't get yourself kicked out of the store, but the best way to judge compost is to actually feel and smell what's inside the bag. Compost should be dark brown and should smell and feel like soil. Avoid anything that smells rotten. Read the ingredients, too. Look for as diverse a range of ingredients as possible, including animal manure and leaf mold. And avoid buying stuff that's basically bark, or has ingredients including biosolids or inert ingredients. Lastly, make sure the bag doesn't feel like a sack of cement.

Beyond that, grab a box of your favorite organic fertilizer. People might try to sell you on "veg" and "flowering" fertilizers. Nitrogen (the first number in the list of three on any fertilizer) is bumped up during grow time, while potassium (the third number) usually increases for flowering. Truthfully, a balanced organic fertilizer is fine for the entire season. Sprinkle a handful around the base of the plant every few weeks or whenever you remember.

A Support System

It's hard to imagine now, but those adorable babies have a lot of growth ahead of them. By the end of their life, they actually add a few pounds to those branches in sticky flowers, making them prone to flopping over or snapping in a sudden gust of wind or an early rain. For that reason, they'll benefit from having a little something to lean on. It's always best to do this at planting time, so that you don't break all your branches later, trying to shove them into openings.

While I never advise people to use those flimsy tomato cages when they grow tomatoes—the vines quickly overpower them, and you've got a mess of bent metal and snapped branches before the season is over—tomato cages are actually perfect for your weed, provided you're following my tips and not trying to grow the biggest plants you possibly can. They come in a few gauges; opt for the heavier-duty ones if you have a choice. And that should do the trick. Just shove them in the ground (or in the container), surrounding your plant, at planting time.

If you are a fussier gardener than me and you like to tie branches to the support as they grow, be sure to keep ties loose—they can cut into plants as the branches grow.

Vegetative and Flowering—Say What?

Geared toward indoor cannabis "gardens," pot resources traditionally make a whole bunch of fuss about vegetative and flowering states. People say things like, "I'm vegging my plants," to describe the part of the season before flowers form. This is part of the weird cannabis-only lingo that makes growing pot seem shrouded in mystery and seemingly out of reach. I've never thought of any of the plants in my garden as being in a "vegetative" or "flowering" state. They're just growing.

The closest similarity I can think of is comparing cannabis to a determinate tomato. For my nongardeners: Tomato varieties are either indeterminate or determinate. Indeterminate varieties continue growing, flowering, and fruiting until the plant gets hit by frost. Determinate tomatoes, on the other hand, stop growing taller at a certain point and stop pushing out new leaves. At this time, they turn all their attention to flowering. The fruit forms all at once, and it ripens all at once. No more growing. The end.

Cannabis is much like a determinate tomato. It grows first, and flowers second. But dividing the whole season into two, pre- and post-flowers, seems arbitrarily divisional. At no point does it feel like a switch has been flipped. It's a gradual and natural process. But with an indoor pot grow, flipping a light switch is exactly what happens. Growers reduce light to induce flowering. They're approximating a summer solstice, but it happens all at once. If you're growing your plants outside, this switch flipping happens naturally. Daylight gets longer and longer until summer solstice, when the hours of daylight gradually—gradually!—diminish. No need to flip a switch. No need to play God. And no need to refer to "vegging" your plants. They're just growing. And then flowering. As plants do.

opposite
Handmade in Los Angeles, the Toki Bubble Trellis from Terra Trellis supports growing cannabis while adding a colorful and sculptural touch to the garden.

Is My Kid Going to Get High?

Cannabis only becomes psychoactive when it's decarboxylated, or science speak for "burned." It has zero psychoactive potential in its raw form. So, if my baby, or your baby, or anyone's baby wanders into my garden and nibbles on a stalk, leaf, or flower from my cannabis plant, nothing is going to happen. I'm much more concerned about the eight *Euphorbia characias* I have planted as part of my landscaping, as the sap causes blindness.

opposite
Use bypass pruners (or scissors, even) to snip the main stem once it is several nodes of growth tall. Many growers talk about three being a magic number. Here I've waited until five, and I'd say my plants are pretty magical.

Pruning

Pruning refers to cutting a plant to control its size, encourage branching, or redirect growth. Left unpruned, a pot plant grows like a Christmas tree—tall and pointy. It forms one main cola (flower cluster). I completely understand the appeal of leaving the plant to do its thing. You're thinking, "A giant bud? Maybe *this* will be the thing that finally impresses my older brother." But I advise against it. A giant bud will be much more susceptible to mold and mildew come harvest time. That density makes it harder to dry and cure. A few careful snips go a long way in creating a much more manageable and worry-free harvest. And if you've heard anything about complicated pruning techniques, just relax. Those are much more applicable to indoor grows, where growers are attempting to make sure static overhead lighting reaches every leaf evenly. Outdoors, a dynamic sun will make sure your plant receives light, and you can have a much less heavy hand.

At the bare minimum, you'll want to snip the top of the plant (known as the terminal bud) when the plant has three pairs of leaves growing along the main stem. Cut just above that third set of leaves. The cut directs the plant to split, forming two smaller branches rather than one big one. Wait until each side branch grows another three sets of leaves and snip again. Truthfully, that is all you need to do. You can put the shears down and walk away from the plant.

Keep an Eye Out for Flowers

following
Keep your eye on those "armpits" to see the first sign of flowering. The female flowers appear as strands of hair (left) while the males' are tight balls (right).

Sometime after the summer solstice, when the light naturally decreases, your cannabis plants will begin to flower. It's an awesome moment the first time you spot one. Even though I made a big to-do about not obsessing over "vegetative" or "flowering" states (it sounds so clinical!), it still means something

5
4
3
2
1

female
flower

male
flower

to see your plants reach this milestone. You've nurtured them into lush green bushes, and now you know that things are about to get wild.

Plant Sexing

Cannabis flowers first appear in the plant's "armpits," or more technically, in the nodes along the main stem. It's at this early, pre-flowering stage that you can decipher the males from the females and get rid of the males to ensure that your finished product will be seed-free.

Telling flowers apart is surprisingly simple and unexpectedly hilarious. Female flowers shoot out delicate hairs, known as stigma. Males flowers begin as round, ball-shaped sacks. Yes, the males actually have balls. It's that easy.

Don't Panic

Having male plants is not a crisis situation. Yes, one male plant packs enough pollen to inseminate a neighborhood's worth of female plants (or so the story goes), but this doesn't happen anytime soon. Plants have a whole journey of growth ahead of them, and males don't burst open for at least a month, if not more. Most people send the males to the compost sooner rather than later to minimize spending excess resources on them. I like to let mine hang out for a while.

Fun with the Boys

Here are a few fun things you can do with male cannabis plants:

Juice 'em

I'm not going to make a bunch of yet-to-be-proven claims about the medicinal power of raw cannabis leaves, but let's just say that those claims are out there. At the very least, it's entirely safe to add these dark green leaves to your morning smoothies.

Make babies

Backyard breeding is totally unnecessary but a whole lot of fun. If you have males and females of the same cultivar, you can cross them, produce seeds, and save on that expense next year. Or, you can cross males and females of different cultivars

right
Throw male plant leaves into the juicer and combine with beets, carrots, an apple, and ginger. I can't tell you it'll cure your ailments, but it certainly can't hurt.

and play the cannabis lottery, seeing what surprises are in store for you next growing season.

If you're going to breed, be sure to isolate the males eventually. They're fine hanging out coed for a while, but when the male flowers start looking like a miniature bunch of swollen bananas, it's time to send them away. I've seen them kept in closets and sheds—they don't need to thrive, they just need to live long enough to have their flowers open. In fact, you can hack the male down to just a branch or two—minimizing the amount of pollen that will burst—and shove it in the garage and water it once a week.

following
One way to isolate your males without any risk of accidental pollination is to hack a branch and put it indoors, in water, just like a flower. It'll continue to grow and develop, forming flowers all within the confines of your home.

When the flowers open, a yellowish white dust of pollen coats the male leaves (and everything nearby). Males and females are likely ready to mingle at the same time, meaning you can use a paintbrush to transfer the pollen straightaway

Blueberry
x
Mango

opposite, clockwise from top left

Male flowers open, releasing a dusting of whitish yellow pollen on everything in sight.

Gather pollen on a paintbrush or shake it into a container.

Make absolutely certain to hang labels from the branches you've selectively pollinated, so you can remember where to fish for seeds a few weeks later.

Make sweet cannabis love by coating the female flowers with pollen.

to the swollen puffballs of female flowers. Alternatively, you can shake the pollen into a dry, sealed container and pollinate at your leisure. You can selectively brush just a few flowers and leave the rest of the crop seed-free. Hang a label from pollinated branches so you know where to expect to find seeds. Be certain not to harvest those branches, leaving them to mature fully on the stalk. A good rule of thumb is that seeds are mature two to three weeks after you harvest your seedless flowers (see page 175 for information on when to harvest). If you're uncertain, use your fingers to fish a few out from their buds and make sure that most are darkly colored. Store seeds in a cold, dark place, like in the freezer, and they should remain viable for many years.

right
Some growers remove fan leaves as the flowers reach ripeness, but there is really no need.

left
Cannabis leaves play with white sage, chocolate cosmos, and purple gooseneck loosestrife.

opposite
There's not much to do as you sit back, relax, and wait for your weed to ripen.

Leave Those Fan Leaves Alone, Mostly

Every grower has an opinion on what to do with fan leaves—those icons of cannabis culture—as the plant grows. Some people swear by removing them to allow more sunlight in, but this is generally more of an indoor-growing technique. Others say you must remove them to trick the plant into focusing on the flowers. I'm not sold. Plants evolve the way they do for a reason. I'm apt to trust evolution and let the plants hang on to their leaves for photosynthesis, sun protection, or whatever other brilliant reason they might have for existing. By the time you near harvest, many of the fan leaves will naturally be yellowing. Some might fall off. Not to worry—it's just a sign that the plant is now indeed focused fully on her flowers.

That isn't to say you can't remove a few and have fun along the way. I find cannabis leaves to be sheer perfection in floral arrangements.

The Waiting Game

You've reached the part of the growing season where there isn't much to do besides keep your plants watered and watch the magic happen. This is my favorite part of the season, when the changes happen fast and furiously, flowers growing gaudier and smellier by the day. Congratulations—you've just grown weed.

Chapter 7

Harvesting, Drying, Curing, *and* Trimming

Growing is only half the journey.

Though I'd argue that it's about the journey, not the destination, the end goal of cannabis gardening is a usable, smokable flower that has dried evenly, with as little non-resinous plant matter as necessary. You're after a smoke that isn't harsh, tastes great, and gets you high. For that to happen, you need to know when to harvest, how to dry the flowers evenly, what parts to remove, and how to properly store your stash so that it gets refined in flavor and stays preserved.

It turns out that the growing part is only half of the equation, and that the real brunt of the labor comes afterward.

Historically, I've not enjoyed crops that need a lot of care after harvest. Really, my beef is with quinoa. It was among the easiest garden crops I've ever grown—drought-tolerant and fuss-free—until harvest, and then I found out that I was anything but done. First came the drying, which was really a cakewalk in comparison to the threshing and winnowing that followed. Do you even know what *threshing* and *winnowing* mean? I didn't. *Threshing* removes something from its stalk, and *winnowing* separates seeds from all the chaff. Threshing is relatively simple: I rubbed the stalks between my hands, and all the seeds and chaff fell into big bowls I'd placed beneath. Winnowing was more of a disaster. I set up a fan with a large baking sheet in front of it. As the seeds were heavier than the chaff, I was able to drop handfuls of seeds and chaff in front of the fan. The seeds fell onto the pan and the chaff blew away. Unfortunately, I did this all indoors. There is no "blew away" indoors. A powdery layer of quinoa chaff dusted every surface in the room, and I needed my inhaler, having induced an asthma attack from breathing in all of that particulate matter. At the end of the day, I had half a paper grocery bag full of quinoa, and I decided that this was one crop I'd happily leave to the farmers.

Growing Weed Is Like Child-rearing

Though I've likened growing pot to growing determinate tomatoes and quinoa, the best metaphor for someone new to growing weed might be raising children. When my baby was brand spanking new, everyone told me to follow my instincts. I felt hugely intimidated by this advice. I spoke to a friend, a woman who is both a nurse and an anthropologist, about my reaction to that advice. She explained that instincts have actually been studied, and they amount to experience. It's a very tall order to tell a new mother to trust her instincts when she doesn't have experience being a mother. Instincts build over time. And that's precisely what happened. By a few months in, I could filter through the input—the instructions, the tips, the advice—and I just had a growing internal sense of knowing what my baby needed.

Weed is similar. Everyone has an opinion on the best way to do every part of the process, especially the harvest and drying. But at the end of the day, you're going to learn your plants. You're going to touch them and smell them. You're going to grow some weed. It's going to be pretty good weed, and everything is going to be OK.

There's a moment in the weed growing process that at first felt really similar to the quinoa debacle. There's all this mystery around growing weed, largely because it's been done indoors or in hiding for so long, but when you grow outside, you realize that it's not actually that hard. Seeds sprout easily. So long as you give them some love and attention (and water and sun and decently draining soil), it all goes really well. You're like, "No wonder it's called weed!" as you pat yourself on the back and wonder if you should actually be a pot farmer for a living.

Then you realize what's headed your way with the post-processing.

The farmers you meet tell you you're going to stink up your whole neighborhood and then your whole house. They introduce a whole new set of terms to your world: *bucking* and *burping* and *trimming*. You fall deep into online weed forums of indoor growers detailing their drying and curing setups, which all involve carbon filters and additional expensive equipment. You cancel your trip to the East Coast because you realize that you're going to have to be monitoring your weed for mold for a few weeks. Your husband tells you that your work is beginning to impact his life in uncomfortable ways and requests, if at all possible, that he not go to work every day smelling like he just hotboxed.

You have a moment. You make frantic phone calls to all the home growers you know, asking them if they'd like to dry your weed for part of the harvest, since you don't really smoke weed anyway. And then you pull yourself out of it, and you say, Johanna—you've got this. *Come on.*

But, thank God—you're about to learn that it's really not so hard. Yes, there is some post-processing. But here's the good news: Because you're only growing a few plants in your backyard, this is not the nightmare that large-scale growers face. You don't need to hire a crew of trimmers; you probably don't even need to clear out a room in your house. Depending on how much your husband resents the project, you might not need a filter to mask the smell. If you time it right, you probably even can take that trip east. And you certainly won't need your inhaler this time around.

Set Up the Drying Room

Before you make any cuts, you need to know where you're going to hang your plants. Drying is crucial. You goal is to have a steady dry that takes between ten days and two weeks in a room with minimal temperature fluctuations. During this time, your weed loses its water content while retaining cannabinoids and terpenes. Optimal drying conditions are a dark room with temperatures that stay between 60°F and 70°F (15.5°C and 21°C), and humidity that hovers between 50 and 65 percent. These ranges are wide, representing the different levels various experts swear by. I've found there to be some wiggle room. A dip or spike here and there won't hurt anything. Depending on your climate and the conditions in your drying room, you might need to take actions to either speed up or slow down the dry. In incredibly hot and arid regions, like the Southwest, a speedy dry degrades your cannabis quickly, so adding humidity with a humidifier is key. In dank, cooler regions, like the Pacific Northwest, a crop that doesn't dry sufficiently can go moldy, hence it can be necessary to speed up the dry with a dehumidifier and a fan.

A garage, basement, shed, or closet is usually just the spot. With a little nudging from a humidifier or dehumidifier or fan or heater, you can likely adjust your conditions as necessary. Invest in a cheap temperature and humidity gauge (called a *hygrometer*) and test your different candidates for drying rooms to track what might be the best spot. The location should be clean. If you've got mold issues, find another location, period. Airflow is important, though you don't want gusts blowing directly on the plants. A small oscillating fan pointed away from the plants is sufficient.

opposite
Picture-perfect weed drying. Sadly, this isn't how it played out in real life.

This Is the Ugly Part

In wanting this book to be super beautiful, I intended to dry in a small closet inside my home that I'd cleaned out for this precise purpose. Simple white walls, twine strung from hooks, a burlap drop cloth to catch any debris—it was pretty. It was most certainly how Martha Stewart would dry her weed.

But the house smelled. A lot. I mean, I thought it smelled awesome. But my husband, the less fun one, wasn't thrilled. So, I moved the entire operation down to an unfinished basement that holds storage and laundry. I bought a standalone wardrobe from Target and added a few extra dowels to hold more weed. Not a single tool was required. It did the job perfectly. But my drying room looks like anyone else's: ugly.

Consider the amount of room it will take to dry your harvest. You'll need enough space to hang branches. They can absolutely be close together but shouldn't be touching, or perhaps just barely. You can hang lines from walls or buy something as simple as a freestanding drying rack (or two).

Lastly, be prepared for the smell. Perhaps this is a 100 percent nonissue for you, but just be advised that the room where the weed hangs will smell pungent as the crop dries. But rest assured—it goes away entirely once the flowers are jarred and stored. The only way to truly mitigate the odor is with the combination of an inline fan outfitted with a carbon filter. You can find both online or at your local hydroponic or grow store. They'll run you anywhere from a hundred dollars to several hundred, depending on how big a space you're needing to filter. The fans are loud. The setup, unless mounted to the ceiling, is a bit precarious. I didn't want to risk my toddler's precious digits finding their way into the fan, which is one of the reasons I opted out of using one.

following spreads
In each of these flowers, about half the stigmas have died back and turned brown, while the other half remain white and supple. These plants are ready for harvest. Also note that fan leaves protrude from branches. Sugar leaves are smaller and grow directly out of the flowers themselves.

Approaching Harvest

Most cannabis ripens fully between August and November. You'll notice that your plants get smellier and stickier. They start to look alien. Things are moving in the right direction. People have different ways of telling when their pot is ripe. Often people suggest using magnification to tell if trichomes—the mushroom-like resinous glands that coat flowers—have changed from clear to milky. I bought a jeweler's loupe for a few bucks and had a good time looking at the trichomes close-

up—trippy! But here's the thing: 3-D magnification of trichomes has revealed that milkiness changes on vantage point, meaning what looks cloudy from one angle can be completely clear from another. So, buy the magnification if you want to have a little fun, but not because you need to. By the way, if you'd like to see amazing macro 3-D photography of weed, visit the work of Erik Christiansen, aka @erik.nugshots.

Harvest day! I'm just a little excited to have reached this milestone.

Ultimately, there are two metrics I like—one because it's generally accurate, and the other because I like how it sounds. Also, when in doubt, wait another week.

1. The Stigma Method

Harvest when half the stigmas (those little hair-like strands) are amber and half are still white. Yep, it's that simple.

2. The Squeeze-the-Nug Method

Give the flowers a pinch. If they feel spongey, they're not ready yet. Once they've firmed up, you're ready to go.

What to do with fan leaves

Some growers make a big to-do about removing fan leaves before they harvest. Others don't. And in any case, many fall off naturally as the season comes to a close. You won't need them for the finished product, so it's totally reasonable to take them off. No equipment is needed—just use your fingers to snap them off. However, leaving them on has an added benefit if you live in an extremely arid climate and are concerned about insufficient humidity during your drying process. Freshly harvested plant material adds moisture in the air, so leaving on fan leaves can help slow down the drying process. In my Bay Area climate, I have success with both methods. Since I like to err on the side of a slower dry, I tend to keep them on, and I need no additional humidifier or dehumidifier to stay between 60 and 65 percent humidity. Just be sure to remove any leaves that are moldy, yellow, or otherwise look like they're at the end of their rope.

Forget the flushing

If you've read about indoor cannabis cultivation, you've heard about growers "flushing" their plants, meaning they flood them with water several weeks before harvest to ensure that any excess amount of nutrients and minerals are flushed away, preventing any impact on the harvest's ultimate flavor. If you've followed my

opposite
Harvest by cutting flower-lined branches into pieces measuring about a foot or two long (30 to 60 cm). It's a fine idea to give your flowers a once-over as you harvest. Check for any dark spots, which might be mold or rot. Prune those out aggressively and dip your shears in alcohol before making more cuts.

method of growing, you planted your plants into well-amended soil, full of compost and not too much else. There is no risk of a buildup of nutrients—especially synthetic ones—and you can absolutely skip this step. Just pretend you've never heard of it.

Harvest Time

Unless you have massive tree-like cannabis plants, it's a fine idea to harvest all of the flowers at once. Farmers and serious growers harvest before sunrise, as sunlight begins the release of volatile terpenes and makes things stickier. It's a-OK to harvest after the sun rises, but try to do it in a cooler part of the morning. If you have managed to grow enormous weed plants (we're talking you need a ladder for harvest), consider snipping outermost buds first and giving the inner ones another week to be bathed in sunlight and ripen.

While you pluck individual tomatoes off their vine, leaving the rest of the plant in place, that's not the case with weed. You're going to harvest entire branches that will be topped or lined with flower clusters. An easy length to work with is usually about a foot or two long (30 to 60 cm). You'll hang the branches to dry, which, in addition to just being a really efficient setup for drying, also helps keep the dry slow and steady, as branches are filled with moisture that slowly dries

right
Cut in a way that creates hooks from which to hang and dry your plants.

opposite
Place your harvest onto a clean tarp.

out. You can either chop your plant at the base and cut smaller sections from there, or cut branch by branch. While there's no right way to chop a plant, there are a few things you can do to set yourself up for success. The first is to lay clean tarps next to your plants. Your chopped branches go straight on the tarp, keeping the harvest clean. And you can easily bundle the bounty up and take it straight to your storage area. The second trick is to chop your plants in a way that creates ready-made hooks that hang easily onto storage lines. Instead of cutting branches off from the main trunk or stem, try to include a small section of that trunk to create a V to hang on a line. And don't worry if your hooks aren't perfect or don't happen every time—clothespins are cheap and do the job, too.

Keep your cultivars on separate tarps, and make sure each tarp is labeled with a piece of masking tape. Be ruthless about labeling. No matter how much you could tell the weed apart in the ground, you won't have that same ability as they all start to dry. Before you start drying, you may wish to trim the flowers. See page 189 for more information on trimming.

To the Drying Room We Go

following
I use hangers on a wardrobe to increase my drying area exponentially. A magnetic hygrometer lets me easily track where I'm at with temperature and humidity. I play around with trimming some flowers and leaving others untrimmed. It depends on my mood. Here, Blueberry Muffin is left untrimmed, while Mango is manicured. No matter what, though, each hanger has a label and holds only that particular cultivar. It helps to keep trimmed and untrimmed on separate hangers so you can closely monitor how individual branches are drying.

Hanging is the ideal method of drying for several reasons. First, it's easy logistically. It's an efficient use of space. Quick trick: If you want to create even more space than just the hanging lines or racks, add hangers and hang from them. Voilà, you just created exponentially more hanging room. Hanging branches also prevents buds from getting smooshed and being slightly sad-looking and less impressive to your friends. Also, maintaining that connection between the flowers and moisture-filled branches allows for a smooth and steady dry.

Expect an uptick in the room's humidity for the first few days, as freshly harvested plant material starts to dry. Adjust your accoutrements (dehumidifiers and fans) accordingly to keep conditions in check. From here, you mostly sit back, smell the smells, and watch the transition.

When is cannabis dry?

A properly dried flower has minimal amounts of chlorophyll and maximum retention of cannabinoids and terpenes. It'll taste good. Storing your cannabis when it's still too wet causes problems with mold, and storing when it's too dry will result in a harsh smoke with less flavor. Let's make sure you know how to tell when you're ready to move on to the next step.

Blueberry
Muffin
10-4

Mango
10-4

If you're very tight on space, you can buy an herb drying rack and pop buds on there to dry. They will be flattened on one side, which is only a big deal when trying to impress your friends with the weed you grew. Keep in mind that when buds are disconnected from their branches, they dry much more quickly, so be sure to check them often.

With proper temperature and humidity conditions, your crop will be dry in ten to fourteen days, but it's a good idea to check your plants every day. Give the nuggets a squeeze and bend a few branches, just to better gauge the progression. When sufficiently dry, flowers should have a little crunch to the touch. Some farmers say it should sound like squeezing popcorn. Others say to make sure it bounces back from being lightly squeezed. It's too moist if it's still really squishy. But really, you need to bend the stems that connect the flower buds to the branch. They should break with a crisp snap.

Giving Your Bud a Haircut

Manicuring—also known as trimming—refers to removing the leaves that surround the flowers. Manicuring is important because it ensures a smoother smoke by eliminating parts of the plant that don't have as many trichomes. But the turd-like buds you are used to seeing are trimmed a little more than they need to be, simply because that's the aesthetic preference of today's market. That doesn't have to be your end goal. Trimming is the bane of most growers' existences. It's laborious and monotonous. An entire industry is built on the trimming labor of migrants who can clip for long hours and deliver market-ready buds. But you're growing a few plants for yourself or friends. Trimming is not such a big deal. Dare I say it's something I enjoy.

There are advantages to trimming when the harvest is fresh (known as wet trimming) and advantages to trimming when the flowers are dry. You'll find plenty of people who swear by one way or the other. I encourage you to do a little of both in order to find your preference.

Wet trimming

Trimming right after harvest is a sticky adventure. Trichomes are still wet—they get on your hands, but they also tend to stay stuck to the plants (as opposed to being dry and brittle and more likely to snap off). If you're tight on drying space, wet trimming will greatly reduce the volume that needs to be hung, opening up more room. Wet trimming also shortens the drying time because the flowers have less moisture to pull from without all those leaves, so keep that under consideration. You might want to wet trim if you live in a cooler or more humid climate and are concerned about your flowers taking longer than a few weeks to dry, which can open the door to mold.

opposite
While you'll never see untrimmed buds at a dispensary, it's not a bad idea to store yours in this state. Sugar leaves cluster around dried flowers, protecting those dried hairs—or trichomes—which contain dense amounts of cannabinoids and terpenes.

Dry trimming

Or you could process all the leaves on as the plants dry, helping slow down the process—especially useful in more arid conditions, as the flowers have more moisture to pull from. Once dried, the leaves snap right off with less stickiness. (Careful, though—trichomes can pop right off, too, and we'd like to retain as many of those as possible.)

Trim as you go

But wait—wet and dry are not the only options. Once I discovered what many growers do with their own personal stash—not the stuff headed to market—there was no turning back. Many people dry their weed and then *buck* it (snip the flowers off the stems) and toss it into storage—sugar leaves and all. Those dried leaves, which have now shriveled to surround the buds, serve to protect the flowers while they hang out in storage. When it's time to smoke or gift some, a quick snip of the sugar leaves reveals a pristine bud with picture-perfect pistils. Your friends *oooh* and *ahhh*. Also, you get off easy by not having to devote much time or space to a trim operation.

right
For manicuring buds, I quite enjoy using Chikamasa B-500sf Stainless Steel Scissors myself.

following
Oh, the many choices when it comes to trimming scissors.

CHIKAMASA
UD
CHIKAMASA
UD
43000
ARS CARBON
CURVED BLADE
$ 17.99
4323
ARS CARBON
STRAIGHT BLADE
$ 17.99
4335
ARS STAINLESS
ORANGE SNIPS
$ 24.75
43280
BONSAI SHEARS
TITANIUM
$ 14.50
$ 14.50
43280
$ 12.50
4328
$ 17.99
43000
Cutter
Bee
EK
MADE IN
JAPAN
4323
$ 17.99
43250

CHIKAMASA
4328
BONSAI SHEARS
STAINLESS
$ 12.50
$ 15.95
4330
STAINLESS
$ 13.50
4335
$ 24.75
4331
13.50
Stainless Steel
4331
GIROS CURVE
STAINLESS
$ 13.50
4330
13.50
TAIWAN
43330
GIROS CURVED
TITANIUM
$ 15.95
Titanium
43330
15.95

Trimming supplies

No matter at what stage you manicure your buds, it's important to do so in a dry, clean environment and have the tools to get the job done.

A clean surface

A clean tarp, table, or tray makes a great surface. If you'd like to collect the *kief*—the resinous trichomes that accumulate while trimming and can be sprinkled in joints or compressed into hash (see page 220 for more on kief)—buy a trimming tray with a built-in screen.

Scissors

You need a special pair of narrow-bladed scissors to manicure your weed. There are several options to choose among: some are spring-loaded, some are not; they can have curved or straight blades. People have a lot of opinions, but again, keep i n mind that most growers are trimming copious amounts of weed. The whole event will be less painstaking for you, and thus choosing scissors should be less of a life-altering decision.

Hand cleaner and/or gloves

Trimming is a sticky activity. You think it's no problem until your phone rings and your hands are covered in goo. Most people wear latex gloves as they trim. If you're like me and can never seem to keep gloves on, make sure you have a bottle of isopropyl alcohol nearby. Better yet, skip the latex and the alcohol and instead mix a solution of a few tablespoons of sugar with a cup or so (8 ounces/240 ml) of nut or seed oil. The sugar will act as an exfoliant and your hands will be left moisturized and smooth.

Isopropyl alcohol and rags

Scissors get jammed with sticky resin. A rag dipped in alcohol makes cleaning quick and easy.

Curing to Perfection

Curing refers to the second phase of drying, in which moisture continues to draw from the center of the bud toward the outside, retaining the volatile compounds and leaving you with evenly dried buds. Just like with drying, a nice, slow cure makes for the smoothest bud. Most people consider their cannabis to be curing for two weeks to a month. Expect the flavor to get less grassy and more cannabis-y the longer you cure. Some growers don't dip into their stash for a full year.

Manicuring 101

Behold: an untrimmed, freshly harvested branch. Always hold your bud by the branch. This prevents squeezing the flowers and damaging them.

Remove any remaining fan leaves, trying to nip them at their connection point. Fan leaves have few trichomes. No need to save them.

Off to a good start. What remains are smaller fan leaves, sugar leaves, and, of course, the buds themselves.

As you get closer in to the buds, snip remaining fan leaves and give sugar leaves a trim, too. As they're covered in trichomes, many people save their sugar leaf trimmings to use in tinctures or butters.

A trimmed bud, ready to hang.

You don't have to trim your weed before drying or storing it. Another option: Store untrimmed weed and manicure it as needed. The upsides are less labor upfront and nicely preserved trichomes that have been protected by dried sugar leaves.

Growers have all sorts of setups for the curing process. Most involve yet another set of supplies, be it Rubbermaid containers, cardboard boxes, or paper bags. Some people swear by porous vessels and others by nonporous.

Save yourself yet another supply run by just using mason jars or stainless-steel canisters with locking mechanisms—two great options for both curing and then storing a small harvest from a backyard grow.

The first step when going from drying to curing is to snip the flowers from their branches and stems, a process known as *bucking*, and get them into jars. Remove as much stem as possible without causing the flower clusters to fall apart.

Fill your jars with your weed. Don't overpack and compress the flowers, but it's fine to fill the jars up. Seal them and walk away. The next morning, you'll want to get into a habit of *burping* them, meaning you release air and let out moisture. You might be surprised to find that those flowers that felt perfectly dried on the branch have regained some moisture content. That's totally to be expected as the flowers continue to pull the last of the moisture out from their depths. If the flowers indeed seem more moist than how you left them, leave the jar lid off for the day. Maybe give the jar a few shakes to move the buds around. At night, reseal, and check again the following morning. Moist again? Lid stays off for the day. Once you find them dry in the morning, consider your weed cured. It's safe to leave the lid on.

If you want to double-check your work with some scientific backup, invest in a digital moisture meter, otherwise used to find leaks in walls, available for $20 or so at any hardware store. You'll stick the pins into the bud and a moisture reading pops up on the display. The ideal moisture for fully dried and cured cannabis is between 10 and 15 percent.

Storing Your Bounty

Gone are the days of plastic baggies stashed in your pocket. You're a grown-up now. If you've already cured your weed in glass or stainless steel, there's not much to do from here; you can just leave it in the same container. Just make sure you've got the proper setup for maintaining the quality of your weed.

You have plenty of options of where to store your weed. Even under the most pristine conditions, it will lose its potency over time and probably get you more sleepy than stoned. Potency is preserved the longest in the fridge or freezer, but proceed with caution: When frozen, trichomes become brittle and break off easily. If you're going the freezer route, give buds time to warm up before you

left
Boveda packets can preserve the humidity in your storage vessels.

If Needed, Add Some Humidity

If you've overdried your buds, as measured with a moisture gauge or as felt by an extremely crumbly, crunchy texture, you'll want to add a humidity pack into the storage vessel. The terpenes and cannabinoids have already likely degraded, so adding humidity won't turn a bad dry into a brilliant one, but it will make for a smoother smoke. Similarly, if you're really happy with the state of your dried and cured bud, you might throw a humidity pack in to preserve the conditions just so. Boveda makes the most popular products. Ideal humidity range in the vessel is between 54 and 63 percent, so buy either their 58 or 62 percent option.

opposite
Take off the lid and give your bud some air those first few weeks. Known as *burping*, this helps refine your weed's flavors.

Amethyst

Mango
Trees
Mango

grind or use them. Also, any excess moisture from not having dried and cured your bud properly can open the door to problems with ice crystals. So be sure you've got a properly dried flower before popping it in the freezer. For the most no-fuss approach, stick by the following guidelines:

previous
Glass mason jars in a smorgasbord of sizes make excellent storage vessels.

The right conditions

Keep it cool Excessive heat (above 80°F/27°C) degrades quality and opens the door for mold.

Not too humid Conditions should be pretty similar to where you dried your cannabis—not moist, not bone-dry.

Dark is better UV light damages the quality. Store your bud in the dark.

Pack it loosely Don't shove buds together. In addition to crushing them, you're likely to increase relative humidity.

Vessels of choice

Glass jars are perfect, but for being clear. This becomes a nonissue if you put them in the dark.

Stainless-steel canisters with plastic seals and locking mechanisms also work fantastically, and there's no need to worry about light.

Vacuum sealing is a great option should you have an excess of weed that you don't want exposed to oxygen (which degrades it) every time you dip in your stash. Consider sealing a part of your harvest that you don't plan on using anytime soon. If you're going to mail weed to your brother, which is totally illegal, you'll also want to vacuum seal. I'm not saying I did this. I actually didn't.

By the way, properly dried and stored weed retains its quality for about four years. I wouldn't know—I like to give mine away.

opposite
From left to right, an Evak container with a lid that forces air out as you push the handle down, a mason jar, and a CVault stainless-steel canister with a locking top.

Mango
evak

The Finished Product

Chapter 8

Though growing weed is more about the journey than the destination, we have nonetheless arrived at our last stop.

I spent the vast majority of high school grounded for being high. My parents swore by a zero-tolerance drug policy that was anything but effective. Fast-forward to our new landscape of legalization, and things are changing in ways I never would have imagined. On more than one occasion (but not every, she'd like you to know), my mom has requested Blueberry Muffin (the most delightful cultivar I've grown) for dessert when she's in town. Yes, my mom asks to smoke my weed. What crazy times are we living in? It's evidence of a massive cultural shift trickling all the way down to the Silver family. Amazing.

When I'm not sharing a joint with my mom, I'm gifting my weed to family and friends. Make sure you know your local laws about how much is permissible to gift at a time. I'm quite enjoying my newfound status as a cannabis supplier. Everyone, from the guy who cuts my mop to the new friend I made at the park, gets some weed.

My brother made a special trip from Brooklyn to smoke my weed. It's taken many decades, but I think I've finally done something in life to impress him. Here he smokes a joint rolled in gold-lined papers.

Joint 101

Whether you smoke it or gift it, it's *absolutely imperative* you learn how to roll a joint.

Supplies

Grinder A small grinder is worth the few bucks to get your weed to the right size quickly and easily.

Cardboard filter tips These prevent your joint from becoming a slobbery mess as you smoke it.

Rolling paper There are so many options to choose from, from unbleached, raw papers to ones lined with 24-karat gold.

Weed A 1½-inch-long (4-cm) nugget (aka a dried flower cluster) or two will be plenty.

Take your pick: Papers range from clear to rainbow.

JAMAICAN HEMP
PAPERS
Skunk Brand
CLASSIC
RAW
NATURAL UNREFINED ROLLING PAPERS
1 1/4 SIZE
ELEMENTS
ULTRATHIN RICE PAPERS
smk
GOLD ULTRATHIN
Pure Hemp
KING SIZE
Smoking
DE LUXE
TRIP2
NOW TREE FREE! THINNER & CLEARER!
ASIATIC COTTON MALLOW ROLLING PAPERS
MODIANO
Club Modiano
UNGUMMED
ELEMENTS
PERFORATED
shine
GOLD ROLLING PAPERS

Step 1

Use a grinder to break your weed into small pieces. Uniform pieces of bud make for an evenly burning joint. Don't overgrind—about ten rotations is enough. Powder doesn't smoke well.

Step 2

Grab your rolling paper and lay it flat, bridging it across the first few fingers of both of your hands. The gluey end—the part that looks like the sticky part of an envelope—should be faceup, pointing away from you.

Step 3

Use a thumb to round the paper, creating a canoe in which to load weed.

Step 4

Fill the canoe with weed. Don't be shy in overfilling it. More is easy to fold than less, and some will spill out as you roll.

Step 5

Using your thumbs against your fore- and middle fingers, begin rolling and compressing the weed into the bottom of the rolling paper.

Step 6

Fold the lower lip of the paper into the joint. It should tuck under the paper smoothly. This is the most crucial, and often most difficult, step.

Step 7

Roll the joint all the way up to the gluey end. Lick the glue, and finish sealing the joint.

Step 8

Take a cardboard filter and coil it up. Roll it smaller than the joint, and as you shove it in one end, it will expand into the size of your joint.

Step 9

Twisting the other end of the joint is optional. It ensures that no weed will fall out. Enjoy!

Step 10

Without the joint in your mouth, light the unfiltered tip while slowly rotating the joint in your fingers. The goal is to create a "cherry," a portion of the joint that is actively burning. Enjoy!

Joint

A rose gold PAX, a rechargeable vaporizer. Grind your flower, pack the chamber full, and inhale.

The traditional way to smoke weed is wrapped in rolling papers. For more information, see pages 210–219.

Vaporizing

Gentler on the lungs than smoking, vaporizing heats your harvest to a lower temperature than fire, activating all the terpenes and cannabinoids without the same level of carcinogens. Make certain you procure a device intended for vaporizing dried flowers rather than one for concentrate, which is an extracted liquid product made in a manufacturing facility. See below for more about extraction techniques.

Homemade Extractions

If you're not going to smoke or vaporize your weed, there are other methods for extraction, aka stripping the cannabinoids and terpenes from the plant material and having them in usable form. Commercial extraction is an always-evolving industry, and because it features expensive equipment (in the case of carbon dioxide extraction) or the possibility of blowing up your home (in the case of hydrocarbon gases like butane and propane), we're skipping those and moving right along. The others, all centuries-old techniques, are totally suitable to try at home.

Kief/hash

To consume the potent part of the plant—nothing but the resinous trichomes—some people collect kief and make hash. *Kief* refers to the blonde-ish powder of trichomes that separate from the plant either as a byproduct of manicuring or grinding weed, or on purpose (to make hash).

Kief can be used as is and sprinkled into joints; many weed grinders come with a small screen that automatically collects any kief that amasses as you grind your weed. When pressed and heated, kief becomes *hash*. Hash is a brick-like substance that can be smoked alone or added to traditional joints. I'm not going to teach you how to make hash—it's not my bag, baby. There's something about it that makes me feel uncomfortable, like it's just too far for me; I like my doses micro and my delivery method less brick-like. Do I have some internalized stigma around

hash that I might need to work though? Possibly. But until I do, there just seems to be something extra "druggy" about it. Like it was meant to be smuggled. People who love hash *love* hash, and you should learn from them. You can press it by hand, but the most popular ways to make it use dry ice or cold water. If this is appealing to you, go for it. Resources abound (see page 243 for further reading).

Decarboxylating (aka heating) weed frees the THC, releasing its psychoactive effects.

Decarboxylating

Beyond kief and hash, step one with any at-home infusion is *decarboxylating* (or "decarbing") your weed. This process transforms the cannabinoid THCa into THC, releasing the psychoactive effects. Also, if you're after a CBD-rich tincture and have grown a cultivar high in CBD (see page 43), you'll also want to decarb the weed to get the maximum benefit. To decarb your weed, place your chosen amount (sugar leaves left over from trimming work great, too, either on their own or in addition to the flowers) on a baking sheet in an oven preheated to 240°F (116°C) for 20 to 30 minutes. Make sure you've cleared this with any other house dwellers before doing it, as it stinks up the house for a few hours.

Tinctures

A discreet way to consume your weed is to prepare a tincture. A *tincture* refers to a concentrated extract of an herb, which you ingest orally from a dropper placed in your mouth or under your tongue. Or mix it with water or into a beverage (see page 233 for a recipe). It's a centuries-old practice, usually made with alcohol (though glycerin can be used if alcohol isn't tolerated). Tinctures are super simple to make. Alcohol effectively separates the cannabinoids and terpenes while acting as a preservative. What I offer here is a folk method of creating a tincture, also known as the "simpler's method," referring to its imprecise yet totally effective results. You can experiment with how strong you want your tincture to be, using anywhere from less than a cup of weed (approximately 13 grams) to as much as you can fit in a quart-size (1-L) mason jar—again remember that there is no way to know potency without lab testing, so you'll have to experiment.

If you'd like your tincture to be psychoactive, you'll have to decarb the cannabis first. By the way—it's also totally reasonable to make a tincture from weed that hasn't been decarbed. Cannabinoids (remember, there are over one hundred of them) are available in their unheated form, too. The effects (be they appetite-stimulating or anti-spasmatic) just might be less pronounced, and you certainly won't get high. In this case, skip straight to putting your weed in a mason jar with alcohol, as described below.

To make a tincture, soak cannabis in grain alcohol for at least a month. Then strain the liquid through cheesecloth and store it in a cool, dark place.

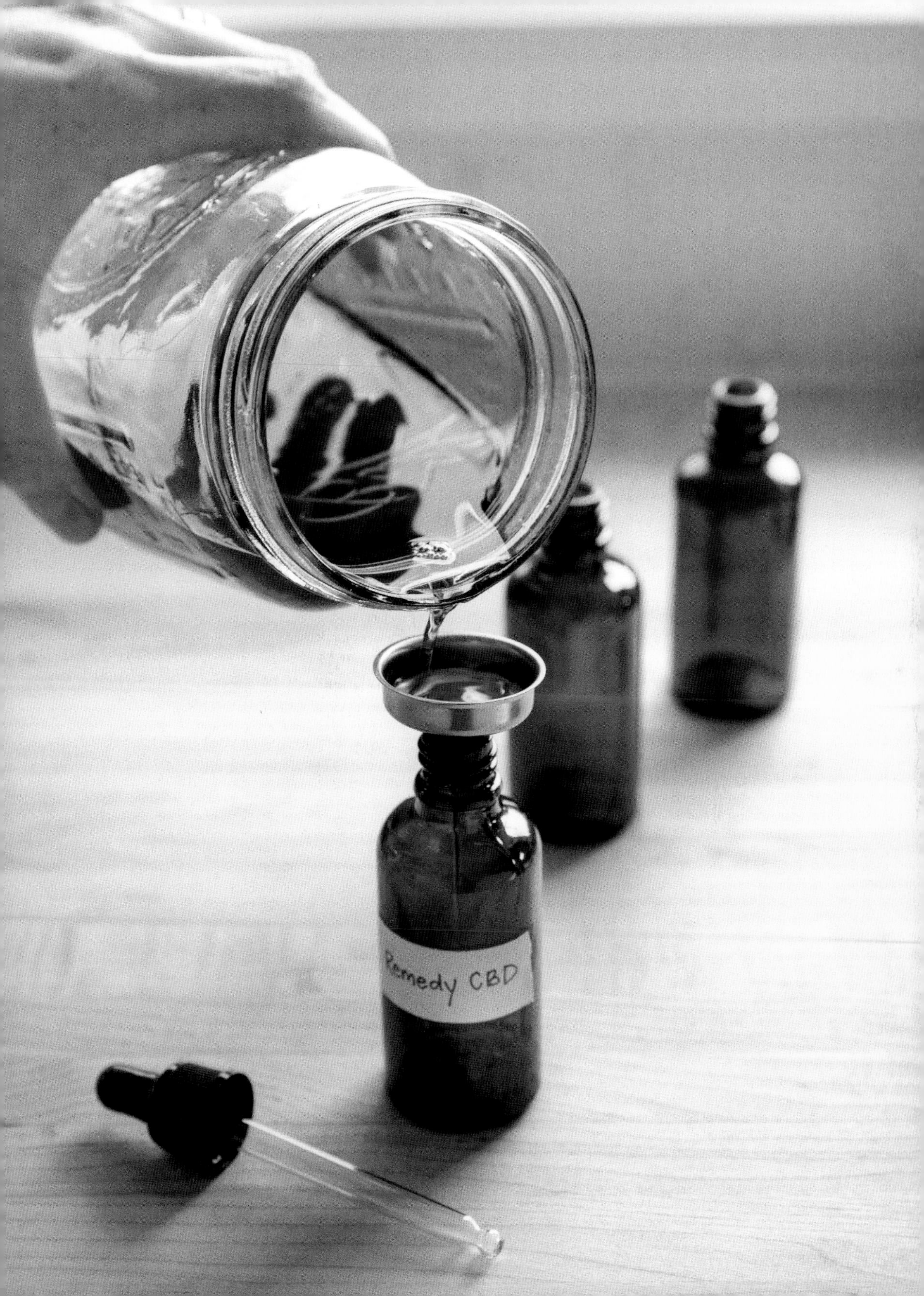
Remedy CBD

CROCK·POT®
Little Dipper®

opposite
Cannabis-infused butter or oil is easy to make and versatile in use.

If you've decarbed, wait until the weed cools. Then put it in a mason jar that fits it comfortably and pour any type of grain alcohol of at least 80 proof or higher over it. Everclear is the gold standard, but it's not available everywhere. I used vodka because I like it. Choose your favorite one! Screw on the cap and store it in a cool, dark place for a month. After that time, filter the cannabis out using a cheesecloth, and funnel the liquid into darkly colored tincture bottles. While some people suggest evaporating the remaining alcohol, this is an unnecessary and potentially dangerous step. Skip it. Your tincture will taste like earthy booze. You might love it and you might hate it. You can always mix it into a glass of water for it to go down the hatch easier (or see page 235 for an infused tisane recipe), but drops under the tongue ensure the most efficient absorption. You'll feel the effects relatively quickly (slower than smoking but faster than edibles). Go slowly as you figure out what effect your new concoction has on your body and mind. So long as your tincture is stored in a cool, dark place, it can last for years.

Infusing oil or butter

Since cannabis is fat-soluble, butters and oils make great solvents for extraction. And similar to tinctures, they're easy to make and versatile. Cannabis-infused oil or butter is what you use to make homemade edibles, like in brownies, drizzled on popcorn, in salad dressing, or in any recipe that calls for oil or butter (see page 236 for cannabis-infused chocolate sauce). Just like with tinctures, you'll want to decarb your weed first to get the full effect. Decarb 1 cup for this recipe. Next, mix your decarbed weed with 1 cup (240 ml) of coconut oil (or butter or ghee or almond oil or olive oil—whatever you want) in a slow cooker set to between 220°F and 240°F (104°C and 116°C) for 3 hours. Afterward, strain the oil into a glass bowl, running it through a cheesecloth to remove plant material. You can store your infused oil in the fridge or the freezer. Make absolutely certain it's labeled, and start with very, very small doses, like ¼ teaspoon (1.25 ml), to see how you're impacted. Remember that it can take up to two hours to feel the effect, so make sure it's been that long before you reach for more. Infused butter or oil is perishable—it will start to degrade after two or three months. It's still usable, but you might notice a change in flavor or potency. To be safe, use it within a year and a half.

following (left)
Cannabis-infused butter mixes with beeswax and dried lavender on its way to becoming salve.

following (right)
Once strained, the salve is quickly poured into small canisters, where it will harden.

Salve

I like to gift my cannabis in its raw flower form, but perhaps you'd like to try your hand at salve-making to see if it helps you and all your friends with your tired,

All-Clad

Salves are used topically to treat skin conditions.

aching muscles. Salves are ointments used to protect or heal skin—no rinsing off required. Start by decarbing your weed. Next, heat 1 cup (240 ml) of coconut oil in a saucepan (ideally a double boiler), add the decarboxylated weed, and stir occasionally for 30 minutes. When you add the weed, you can also add any other dried herbs for scent or medicinal benefit: Calendula, chamomile, lavender, and lemon balm are a few great examples. Filter the mixture through a cheesecloth into a glass bowl and add 1 cup (240 ml) of warmed beeswax. If you didn't opt for dried herbs but still want other smells and qualities, you can add a few drops of your favorite essential oils at this point. Pour into salve containers (tin or glass, both available from a craft store, work great), and let cool. Store your salve in a cool spot where it will remain semisolid and won't continually remelt and resolidify. There are all sorts of claims about cannabis salve, including that it reduces inflammation, helps burns heal, and relieves arthritis. The good news is that you can experiment freely with salves without experiencing any of the psychoactive impacts. You won't get high from a topical application. Having said that, please ask your doctor if you have any concerns about your own condition. Stored properly, salves should last between one and three years.

Regional Perspective

In the kitchen *with* Laurie Wolf

With a decades-long career as a food stylist and food editor in New York City, Laurie Wolf pivoted to cannabis in 2014. She is the author or co-author of several cookbooks, including *Herb*, *Cooking with Cannabis*, *Marijuana Edibles*, and *The Medical Marijuana Dispensary* (with more in the works). Now based in Portland, Oregon, she and her daughter-in-law, Mary, run a baked-goods operation, which sells edibles under the name Laurie + MaryJane. Check it out: *laurieandmaryjane.com*.

You've been in publishing longer than you've been in cannabis, right?

Oh yeah. I was a food stylist in New York. I was a food editor at *Mademoiselle* until they realized that nobody who read it actually ate anything. Then I was at *Child* magazine. Mainly, I did recipe development, but I started out in food styling.

How did you make a turn toward cannabis?

It's basically always been a part of my life. I started using at a pretty youngish age, fifteen or so. I took a few years off to be "a responsible parent," but then I was like, fuck it, and started smoking pot. I smoke a considerable amount now. I eat a lot of edibles. I don't drink at all. I have a seizure disorder. I was on medication for years. Now I'm off all my medication and I just use cannabis to manage it. It's changed my life. I'm a believer. I've seen a bunch of people switch from opioids to cannabis to manage severe pain. I think this plant is a miracle, and I'm not a miracle person.

Have you always been this open about your love of cannabis?

Yeah. Pretty much. I was a teenager during the hippie times. My pot use was actually pretty benign compared to my other drug use.

What's been the hardest part about cooking with weed?

It took some time to be able to dose properly. When I started some years ago, there was no information about potency of the cannabis you bought. Some places sold trim, which usually wasn't super potent or expensive, so I started experimenting with that. I'd roll a joint with it and get a feel for it. If I could smoke the whole joint, I knew it wasn't so strong. If I could only take a few hits, I knew it was stronger. Experiential information was all I had.

But cannabis has gotten way more potent. There were a bunch of times where I'd taste something a few times while I was cooking with an infused oil—not a spoonful; just, say, licking a finger—and I'd have to go to bed. I was getting super high.

Once things got legal, we started working with a lab. I have fewer mistakes with potency, but you know, I still have my moments.

I'd love to hear some of your tips for the home cook.

OK, first can we establish that there's really no such thing anymore as indica or sativa. Do you know that? You know that, right? [Yes, I know that. And you can see page 33 to revisit why.]

[OK, back to tips. Back to the brownie-baking.]

Right, the brownie. The Rice Krispies treat. That's just what people know. I find that a lot of people aren't interested in eating something sweet. They're taking it medicinally, and they don't want to have to eat a brownie.

I always suggest infusing cannabis into coconut oil. That way, it can double as a topical, so right away, you have two applications. We've found that coconut oil retains a higher potency than infusing into butter. So, for our edibles company, we'll infuse coconut oil and then infuse that into butter for our baked goods.

And beyond the baked goods, what are some no-fuss uses for that infused oil?

So long as a recipe calls for some type of fat, it's easy. Just replace some of it with the oil. The easiest thing you can do is add a cannabis-infused coconut oil into a smoothie. Here's your recipe:

- 1½ cups fresh fruit
- ¾ cup whatever type of milk you like—cow, almond, oat, whatever
- 1 frozen banana
- 2 teaspoons infused oil

Blend it. The oil emulsifies. Serves two.

[I'm telling people that, unless they use a lab, all potency calculations are approximate and to use a teaspoon as a starting dose. Do you approve?]

Oh yeah. A teaspoon is standard. Half of one if they're extremely conservative.

Any last tips?

Don't use the infusions in anything above 340°F (175°C). Through our lab tests we find that the most important cannabinoids and terpenes are retained at that temperature or lower. So if you're sautéing, add your infusion at the end, away from the heat.

Eating and Drinking with Cannabis-Infused Goodies

Passionate about cannabis and cooking, Penny Barthell (see page 88 to revisit her garden) is on a mission to educate the canna-curious about how to safely and comfortably consume weed in a way that feels right for them. Her startup, Let's Sesh, offers workshops to Bay Area adults who are new to cannabis or revisiting it after time away. Learn more at wonderingaboutweed.com. I'm delighted to have a reason to play with her in the kitchen.

left to right

Penny and I are both suckers for the same herbs: lemon verbena and mint.

A dropper of tincture added to the herbs. If you've got fresh cannabis flowers growing, add one! It won't add any psychoactive effects, but you'll certainly get a hefty dose of terpenes and raw cannabinoids.

Terp Tisane

While it's totally legit to just open your mouth and squirt some down the hatch, alcohol, well, burns. For that reason, a great way to step it up is to mix your tincture into another drink. It could just be water, but let's get fancy. Enter the tisane—fresh herbs steeped in boiling water (I'm not calling it tea, as true tea—green, black, white, and oolong—all comes from one plant, *Camellia sinensis*. The rest is herbal tea or, more accurately, tisane).

Ingredients

A generous handful of fresh, clean herbs. Any will do. Great choices include chamomile, lavender, lemon verbena, and mint.

Get to it

- Place herbs in your mug or teapot and cover with boiling water.
- Steep for 4 minutes and then strain.
- Add several drops of your tincture and enjoy.

Strain after steeping and enjoy an infused tisane.

Perfect (Vegan) Chocolate Sauce

I have an extreme sweet tooth. So while you can throw your infused oil in a smoothie (see page 233 for that recipe) and take the angle of health nut, I'm still going to be over here, advocating for dessert.

Ingredients

⅔ cup (150 ml) water
4 ounces (110 g) unsweetened chocolate, chopped
1 cup (7 ounces; 200 g) granulated sugar
¼ teaspoon sea salt
¼ cup infused coconut oil
½ teaspoon pure vanilla extract

Adding a quarter-cup of infused coconut oil to a homemade chocolate sauce.

Get to it

- Combine water, chocolate, sugar, and sea salt into a medium saucepan.
- Place on medium-high heat and bring to a boil, stirring with a whisk.
- Simmer for 1 to 2 minutes until sauce begins to thicken a bit.
- Remove from heat and stir in butter, infused oil, and vanilla extract, whisking until smooth.
- Cool until warm, then blend for a few seconds using a hand blender. This creates a smooth, velvety texture.
- Use on ice cream or wherever you like your chocolate sauce.
- Store airtight in the fridge for up to a month.

left to right

Infused canna-oil chocolate sauce being poured over vanilla ice cream.

Tasting the goods. Real story: I didn't decarb the weed for this and just cheated by heating weed in coconut oil for about 20 minutes. Turns out that still did the trick. I reorganized every cabinet in my kitchen shortly after this photo was taken.

A Note About Dosing

Calculating the accurate potency of a homemade tincture or oil is impossible without lab testing, period. There is an increasing number of labs that offer potency testing for relatively cheap (under $100), which might be worth it if you really want to know the exact potency of your cannabis, either in flower or extracted form. Steep Hill, for example, has locations in eight states.

Otherwise, it's very much a guessing game. Here's how to get a rough idea:

1

If possible, identify the THC (or CBD) percentage of the weed you are using. For example, my favorite cultivar, Blueberry Muffin, averages 16 percent THC. Of course, depending on the source of your weed, finding this info might be difficult or impossible. It might be listed on the seed packet or available online. Cultivars range from nearly no THC to upward of 25 percent. CBD content ranges from negligible to around 10 percent.

2

Weigh your dried cannabis flower—the amount will likely be in grams. (I use the scale my husband has for his hipster pour-over coffee nonsense.) Multiply that figure by 1,000 to convert it into milligrams.

4 grams x 1,000 = 4,000 mg

3

Multiply that number by the total amount of available THC (in decimal form) to find the amount of total available THC in that weighed amount. So, for 16 percent THC:

4,000 mg x .16 = 640 mg

4

Figure out the amount per a small serving, like 1 teaspoon (5 ml). For example, say you're going to infuse 1 cup (240 ml) of oil with 4 grams of Blueberry Muffin. There are 48 teaspoons in a cup.

640 mg / 48 = 13.33 mg/teaspoon

Or let's imagine we were taking those same 4 grams and making a tincture with 1 cup (8 ounces/240 ml) of vodka. You're eventually planning to pour the 1 cup into an 8-ounce (240-ml) tincture bottle and dispense it with a 1-ml dropper. There are 236.59 ml in 8 ounces.

640 mg / 236.59 = 2.7 mg/1-ml dropper

Note that this is entirely approximate. Some potency is lost in any extraction method, so the 16 percent THC isn't a fully accurate starting point for your calculation. For example, take the tincture—not all of the cannabis would find its way into the final product, as the cheesecloth would certainly absorb some of it no matter how hard you squeezed. Again, approximate. Inexact. Capisce?

What's the right dose?

That varies widely between people. Three mg of THC might go unnoticed by some, while it has my mom convinced she should be making documentary films of whatever is happening in front of her (she shouldn't be). Even more reason to start with a small trial—a few drops or ¼ teaspoon (1.25 ml)—and wait at least two hours before trying more.

Congrats!

I'd like to commend
you on growing what
is likely the oldest
plant under human
cultivation. You're part
of an ancient chain
of human interaction
with cannabis.
I encourage you to
celebrate, reflect,
and if you're like me,
count the days
until you pop seeds
next spring.

Resources

From start to finish, here are some supplies that might help things go extra smoothly.

Growing

Quictent Waterproof UV Protected Reinforced Greenhouse (*quictents.com*): Portable hothouse to give your baby cannabis plants some protection.

Agribon AG-19 Floating Row Cover (*groworganic.com*): Insect control and light frost protection. Another great option for protecting seedlings.

Phylos Plant Sex Test (*phylos.bio*): Kits to determine the sex of plants just days after germination.

Hydrofarm Dirt Pot (*hydrofarm.com*): Flexible, portable, fabric planter.

Terra Trellis Toki Bubble Trellis (*terratrellis.com*): Sculptural support for cannabis plants to grow on.

Manicuring

Chikamasa B-500sf Stainless Steel Scissors (*bighydro.com*): For manicuring flowers.

Heavy Harvest Trim Tray (*bighydro.com*): Catches kief while you manicure.

Drying

AcuRite Humidity and Temperature Monitor (*acurite.com*): An easy way to monitor the temperature and humidity of the drying room.

Storage

Boveda (*bovedainc.com*): Humidity packs to preserve cannabis in storage.

Prepara EVAK Storage Containers (*prepara.com*): Removes air from storage containers to keep cannabis fresh longer.

CVault (*cvaultstorage.com*): Stainless-steel storage containers with airtight locking lids.

Using

PAX (*paxvapor.com*): Vaporizes dried flower.

RAW Natural Rolling Papers (*rawthentic.com*): All of their papers are plant-based with no chalk or dye, and they even have an organic hemp one. Why not go the distance?

Further Reading

Whether you want to dig deeper on the history of the plant or just want to learn how to make better canna-brownies, here are great resources to keep learning.

History and culture

Clarke, Robert, and Mark Merlin. *Cannabis: Evolution and Ethnobotany.* University of California Press, 2016.

Stoa, Ryan. *Craft Weed: Family Farming and the Future of the Marijuana Industry.* MIT Press, 2018.

Cultivation

Deardorff, David, and Kathryn Wadsworth. *What's Wrong with My Marijuana Plant? A Cannabis Grower's Visual Guide to Easy Diagnosis and Organic Remedies.* Ten Speed Press, 2017.

Rosenthal, Ed. *Marijuana Grower's Handbook: Your Complete Guide for Medical and Personal Marijuana Cultivation.* Quick American Archives, 2010.

Rosenthal, Ed, and David Downs. *Marijuana Harvest: Maximizing Quality & Yield in Your Cannabis Garden.* Quick American Archives, 2017.

Stewart, Madrone. *Feminist Weed Farmer: Growing Mindful Medicine in Your Own Backyard.* Microcosm Publishing, 2018.

CBD

Project CBD (*projectcbd.org*): An ideal place to start with all of your CBD questions.

Photography

Erik Christiansen (@erik.nugshots)

Use

Cech, Richo, and Sena Cech. *Making Plant Medicine.* Herbal Reads, 2016.

Hua, Stephanie, and Coreen Carroll. *Edibles: Small Bites for the Modern Cannabis Kitchen.* Chronicle Books, 2018.

Laurie + Mary Jane (laurieandmaryjane.com). Recipes and resources for cooking with cannabis. Oregon residents can also purchase their baked goods locally.

Rosenthal, Ed, with David Downs. *Beyond Buds: Marijuana Extracts—Hash, Vaping, Dabbing, Edibles & Medicines.* Quick American Archives, 2014.

Acknowledgments

To Carole Bidnick, for being equal parts agent and fairy godmother. I'm so lucky to have you in my corner.

To Kitty Morgan, for starting me on this journey.

To Rachel Weill, for being my creative copilot.

To Laura Dozier, for believing in this project and pushing me.

To Nat Pennington, Ben Lind, Johnny Casali, Cyril Guthridge and Anna Petty-Guthridge, Zero and Tilly Nylin, Zak Powers, Daniel Stein, Dan Grace, Stephen Duarte, Nishan Karassik, Mowgli Holmes, Ellen Markham, and Anna Symonds, my weed mentors, who have generously shared their contacts, wisdom, farms, time, and selves. Thank you for letting me in.

To Berkeley Indoor Garden (Jamal!) for the free therapy.

To my Sunset family—Yvonne Stender, Linda Peters, Jim McCann, Amy Machnak, Emma Star Jensen, and Janet Sluis. I hope to cross paths with all of you for the rest of my life.

To Paola Hernández, for being my village.

To Adam, teamwork makes the dream work. I love you so very much.

To Mom and Dad, I accept your apologies for grounding me for most of high school for smoking weed. You see now that it was all research.

About the Author and Photographer

Johanna Silver is a regular contributor to *Martha Stewart Living, Better Homes & Gardens,* and Leafly and is the former garden editor of *Sunset* magazine. She lives with her husband and young son in Berkeley, California. In her garden she grows strawberries—mostly alpine, blueberries, tomatoes, perennial herbs, a little weed, and as many cut flowers as she can possibly fit.

Rachel Weill is a San Francisco Bay Area–based travel, food, and lifestyle photographer. Her work has appeared in *Condé Nast Traveler, Town & Country,* and *Sunset.* Of all the subjects she photographs, she finds farmers and gardeners to be the most inspiring.

Index

S

T

U

Editor: Laura Dozier
Designer: Peter Ahlberg, AHL&CO
Production Manager: Kathleen Gaffney

Library of Congress Control Number: 2019936961

ISBN: 978-1-4197-4276-7
eISBN: 978-1-68335-808-4

Illustrations by Peter Ahlberg

A note on the type: In celebration of the dynamic, varied, and playful nature of cannabis and its growth, this book uses several fonts at various sizes including Plain Regular, Italic, and Bold and Theinhardt Extended Regular by Optimo Type Foundry, Switzerland; GT Sectra Display Light and Light Italic by Grilli Type, Switzerland; and Austin Text Italic, Publico Banner Light, and Styrene A Regular and Italic by Commercial Type, USA.

Printed and bound in the United States
10 9 8 7 6 5 4 3 2 1

195 Broadway
New York, NY 10007
abramsbooks.com